HOW BUILDING THE FUTURE REALLY WORKS

MATS LARSSON

Get the First Chapter of Mats' Next Book for Free

The first chapter of Mats' next book: *The Electromobility Transformation Handbook* is already available. Get it now!

What type of decisions need to be made to move the implementation of electromobility forward. Car companies and utilities clearly have the technical knowledge to move forward, but what decisions need to be made to expand charging infrastructure, power production and grid capacity? What do managers at logistics and industrial companies, or administrators and decision makers in local government need to know to make investments, start projects, or discuss the transformation with business and implementation partners?

Large investments will be needed. Estimates indicate that some countries will need to double power production and others will need to increase it by 50 percent. Utilities will have to invest in all parts of power grids to facilitate a complete change to electromobility.

400,000 Americans were involved in the Apollo program. More are likely, on each continent, to need to participate in the transformation to electromobility. Are You one of them? What do you need to know to do your part of this massive transformation?

The Electromobility Transformation Handbook will be published in the spring of 2024. Get the first chapter free of charge via the address below:

www.getinstitute.com/electromobilitytransformationhandbook

Hire Mats as Presenter and Consultant

Mats is an experienced consultant and presenter with a unique understanding of how technology and business are developed by visionary individuals and companies. He has studied in-depth how government decisions and activities need to interact with company initiatives and be combined with private funding to create the technologies of the future.

To develop the businesses of the future, companies need a picture of the overall development process and their position in it.

For more than 30 years Mats has worked with clients in large and small companies, governments, and non-governmental organizations.

He is available for presentations and consulting assignments.

Contact him via email: mats@getinstitute.com

How Building the Future Really Works

From Information Technologies (IT) and Space Technologies to Power Production and Electromobility — What Society Needs to Take the Next Leap Forward

Table of Contents

1

A Challenging Future

Developing the technologies of the future will not be a straightforward process. Governments must prioritize the most important technologies and systems and invest heavily in their development. Look at the Apollo space program, for example. Neil Armstrong and Buzz Aldrin would not have been able to walk the moon only nine years after JFK's announcement of such a lofty goal if market forces had been solely responsible for development. NASA drove the push for innovation, and they are the reason why the tight schedule was met.

Due to our inability to grasp technology development, the future may not look the way people expect.

The Logic of Development

We have all experienced the technology development of the past. People can access new technologies without having to consider how they came about. Frequently, many new technologies are developed out of sight of the public, and we are only made aware of them as they become mature enough to be applied on a large scale.

Over and over again, we have experienced technical leaps that have surprised us. Now, as we have access to technologies that have become increasingly affordable, it seems logical to assume that the process will continue and that people will be able to use new technologies regularly in the future as well, and that the technologies will gradually become affordable, even cheap.

What could stop this development? Why should it not go on for decades or centuries? Our difficulty grasping abstract concepts like innovation may be the reason behind the confusion that surrounds technology development, the topic of this book. Few decision-makers and experts seem to really understand the resources that are needed to develop new technologies and drive them to maturity, or to understand the time involved.

After all, development seems to be automatic. Once it has started, we get the impression that it continues, propelled by its own inevitability. Technology development all the time creates new business opportunities, and entrepreneurs like Mark Zuckerberg, Jeff Bezos, and Elon Musk will be there to develop attractive offerings, create jobs, make profits, and build fortunes. As a by-product of this process, development continues, people get increasingly well-paying jobs, and affluence spreads across the world, bringing poor people up from poverty. It is a seemingly unstoppable development.

How Growth Has Been Created

It is tempting to believe that development is automatic and that it is bound to continue forever, promoted and amplified by governments, entrepreneurs, and large corporations. Well-known author and analyst of the future Kevin Kelly describes technology development as inevitable in his book *The Inevitable*. In reality, it is not that simple.

Economic growth is created through improved economic efficiency. Innovation and development have been some of the most important tools to achieve this. Technology has helped us reduce the cost of production and distribution, and through this process we have been given numerous products and services that have contributed to economic growth and to making life more comfortable in our modern society.

If we take a closer look at the development of the past decades, they stand out in history as an unusually prosperous period. Since the post-war years, innovation and economic growth have continued through the boom of the 1950s and 1960s. During the stagflation period of the 1970s and 1980s, people experienced a period of slower growth and financial instability, but by the end of the 1980s, development and implementation of IT started to take off while other efforts toward technology development also started to pay back post-war investments.

During the 1970s and 1980s, there was a lot of uncertainty about the future, but this turned into clarity as economic growth suddenly picked up speed and stagflation came to an end. Around the year 2000, heavy investment in the development of computers started to generate efficiency improvements that contributed to economic growth.

In parallel, the development of mobile telephony started in the early 1980s as phone system operators in the Nordic countries, together with Ericsson, built the first mobile phone systems. The first generation of mobile phone technologies was called Nordic Mobile Telephony, or NMT, due to its origin.

As these developments progressed, mobile telephony and computer technologies converged, a trend that was completed with the launch of the iPhone in 2007. IT and communication technologies became ICT, information and communication technologies. The internet and all the information available there could be accessed via smartphones, tablets, computers, and a host of other devices.

Technical development has gained speed in many different industries. In many cases, it has been driven by

ICT. Computers and communication technologies have been used to reduce costs, increase the value of products, and drive economic growth.

There are now 1,500 computer chips in each car, and the importance of processors is rapidly on the increase. By 2030, industry experts estimate that every car will contain three thousand chips, and in electric vehicles, semiconductors will take on increasingly critical functions, such as controlling the charging of batteries and the utilization of energy. Chips are now developed with highly specialized functions. There are semiconductors designed to be used for power electronics, for example to be used in electric vehicles and other areas where chips will have to withstand higher voltage. Processors and the products in which they are critical components have become inexpensive enough that even cheap toys contain one or more chips.

Big Decisions Driving Development

While in many ways this development has benefited humanity, it has also made people complacent. Many believe that the technical advances of the past two or three decades have come about without involvement from human decision-makers except for those who have been developing the technologies. This, however, is not true. Since the Second World War, governments and companies of all sizes have driven this development forward through large-scale decisions.

In the decades following the Second World War, alternative investment opportunities were fewer than today, and the need to drive economic growth and develop strategically important technologies made the decisions relatively easy to make. Governments in all countries realized, for example, that society in the late twentieth century would require significant power, and decisions were made to expand power production and distribution. Alternative technologies were rare, and countries selected those that best suited their needs and circumstances, supporting those utilities with governmental investment.

Developments that had been started before the war were further developed during the war. Advancements had been made that could be utilized and further developed in the post-war period. At the same time, the Cold War created a need to drive the development of strategic technologies that could secure nations against enemy attacks. The American government spent very large sums financing the development of computers, airplanes, space rockets, the internet, and nuclear power, to mention only a few of the focal areas of investment.

The Market Is Seen as the Most Important Driver

The idea that the mechanisms of the market economy are the most important factors behind this tremendous technology development has become increasingly widespread among economists, politicians, business leaders, and the public. According to the key tenets of neo-classical economics, governments should take only a minimal role in technology and financial development. Governments, national banks, and government agencies should create stable markets by controlling the money supply, interest rates, and perhaps supporting technical development at early stages.

Governments Have Important Roles

In reality, the role of governments in technology development has been much more important than many experts and politicians seem to have realized. The late Professor Vernon W. Ruttan of the University of Minnesota studied six examples of technology development (the American production system, airplane technology, space technology, computers, the internet, and nuclear power) over the past two centuries and found that large-scale and long-term government financing significantly contributed to speeding up development in all these areas.

According to Ruttan, our present society would have looked very different in the absence of large-scale and long-term government financing. Many of the technologies that play the most prominent roles would not have become developed to their present level of refinement without huge amounts of government support. In recent decades, the role of governments in the development of key technologies has largely been neglected.

For example, governments in several countries are in the process of making decisions to ban the sales of new gasoline and diesel cars. These processes have been driven forward without considering the investment in, for example, power generation and distribution that will be needed, or the level of technology and business solutions that will have to be developed and implemented for electric vehicle systems to become competitive.

It is probable that, for example, electric road systems will have to be built to make a complete shift to electric vehicles possible. In a study made by Jakob Rogstadius at the Swedish research institute RISE,[1] in which five hundred scenarios for the future electric transport systems were analyzed, all of them depend for their efficiency on the large-scale expansion of electric road systems, motorways, highways, or city streets with power tracks in or on the road surface that will make it possible to charge vehicles while driving. This construction of electric roads on a large scale has not even started.

The Swedish government is planning the electrification of 2,700 miles of the largest roads in Sweden, but some experts believe that at least 4,000 miles will be needed. Larger networks will be needed in Germany, France, and other large countries. Though the first stretches of permanent electric roads are planned, between three and four years will be required to finance, receive building

---

1 Rogstadius, Jakob. "Interaction Effects between Battery Electric Trucks, Electric Road Systems and Static Charging Infrastructure." RISE Nov 2022 (Swedish title: Interaktionseffekter mellan batterielektriska lastbilar, elvägar och laddinfrastruktur).

permission, and plan the construction in detail. This time may be reduced further on in the process, but to build extensive networks of electric roads across the world before 2035, the decision-making and planning processes need to be sped up and large amounts of financing will have to be made available.

The technologies are in their infancy, and several of the companies that have developed them are still start-ups with very little capital available for large-scale development and growth. When I drive around in my part of the world, southern Sweden, I see few signs that electromobility is on its way to becoming implemented on a large scale. This is despite the fact that Sweden is one of the countries that lead this development with more than 10 percent electric cars and an increasing number of electric buses and trucks. Across Europe and in the United States there are about 3–4 percent electric cars, and the number of buses and trucks is minuscule in most cities.

No country, not even the leading country, Norway, has started to prepare for the large-scale implementation of electric vehicle fleets. With 30, 50, or 70 percent electric cars, the demand for electricity will grow tremendously. Elon Musk has said in an interview that countries will have to double power production to facilitate a complete conversion to electromobility.[2]

Believing that it will be possible to ban the sales of

---

2 Slightly more than fifty-nine minutes into the interview at Codecon 2021, Elon Musk was asked by a member of the audience if the power supply will become a bottleneck for the transformation to electromobility. The question and his reply can be listened to here: https://www.youtube.com/watch?app=desktop&v=TcI6FaaDp8g.

new petroleum-fueled cars from 2035 onward can only be described as an example of *hyperthink,* a concept that will be extensively discussed below.

As an example, air regulators in California have decided to ban the sales of gasoline cars after 2035. This decision was made in the fall of 2022. A few weeks later, utilities in California recommended that owners of electric cars not charge their vehicles over Labor Day due to an expected shortage of generation capacity.

Californians have experienced shortages in their power supply for decades, so this may not come as a surprise, but the truth is that with 280 million cars, the United States would need more than 1,000 TWh of electricity, or ninety new nuclear reactors, to charge all cars if all cars were electric. In the coldest weeks of winter, the amount of power needed would increase even further, as the range driven by an electric vehicle goes down in cold temperatures. Some models of electric cars need significantly more electricity at -10 degrees C than at 20 degrees.[3]

---

3 This may seem like an exaggeration, but I bought my first electric car in 2018, a Renault Zoe. I received it at the beginning of February and in the weeks following the delivery a cold spell hit southern Sweden. The normal range in spring or summer temperatures was 300 km, as I found out later. A week after I had received the car, I was going to a three-day meeting close to the Malmö Airport. The round trip from my house to the airport is 150 km. When I drove to the airport the temperature was lower than -10 degrees C, and when I arrived at the hotel, I had less power remaining than the distance needed to drive my car back home and I had to charge at the hotel. At the time this was a challenge, as the hotel did not have any chargers or electricity sockets in the parking lot. I had to drive into one of the frozen flower beds to reach a socket I could use for charging. One year ago, by the end of 2021, I bought a new Renault Zoe. This model loses less of its range in cold temperatures, only perhaps 30 percent, but I have not been able to test it for driving extensive distances in -10 degrees C, because we normally have mild winters in southern Sweden.

1,000 TWh amounts to 25 percent of the present US production of 4,000 TWh per year, which indicates that a significant amount of new power generation capacity will have to be built in the coming decades. The transformation to electric trucks would require a similar amount of electricity as that needed to charge cars, and in the coldest weeks of cold winters, the need for generation capacity increases even further.

Hyperthink is the process of making critical decisions about the future of countries and their citizens without considering the resources or activities needed to go through with them. It is a process where large swathes of the population are carried away in a vortex of wishful thinking, fueled by enthusiastic leaders and experts who have not bothered to investigate the reality of their arguments and decisions.

Hyperthink leads to a situation where there is no structured discussion, where decision-makers, experts, and people in general are carried away by largely unfounded optimism. Despite the unrealistic goals set by decision-makers, not even opponents are able to see through the grave mistakes that are made and put forward counterarguments.

In a decision similar to that made in California, the EU parliament has opted to ban the sales of new gasoline and diesel cars from 2035. There are 245 million cars in the EU, each driven only half the miles that are driven by cars in the United States, which means that some 500 TWh will be needed to fuel them, with more during the winter. An additional 300 TWh will be needed to fuel trucks and buses; this amount is also likely to increase in cold temperatures.

A few countries, like Germany and Italy, have opposed the decision, arguing that cars with combustion engines should be allowed to be sold provided that they are powered by new synthetic fuels. Production of these fuels requires large amounts of electricity. To drive the entire European car fleet on synthetic fuels, or e-fuels, several times the amount of electricity needed to drive battery-electric vehicles would be needed. There is also no large-scale production of synthetic fuels at present. To convert transport systems to e-fuels, power production would have to expand more than what will be needed to convert to electric vehicles.

To change to electric vehicles, in addition to the investment necessary in power generation, countries will have to expand charging infrastructure, build extensive systems of electric roads, and expand electricity grids. In a world where most cars and an increasing share of trucks and buses are electric, all electric vehicles will have to be charged whenever they need to charge, wherever they happen to be. Currently, only a small share of cars is electric.

Forcing all car buyers to buy electric from 2035 will be a completely different proposition compared to the present situation. Electric cars are about 50 percent more expensive than gasoline and diesel[4] cars, they offer some two hundred to four hundred miles on the battery, and charging takes anywhere from ten or fifteen minutes to several hours. Many people without their own dedicated parking spaces are not likely to be able to conveniently charge their cars overnight. To charge all cars on a regular basis, an extensive network of chargers for stationary charging will have to be built, likely complemented by electric road systems.

With electric roads, drivers will not need to stop to charge. It is believed that some shipping routes will require 30 percent more trucks to make up for the transport capacity lost through stationary charging. With electric roads, there are no cables, which means no tripping hazards for drivers and other personnel at loading docks and in parking areas. Some logistics companies in Sweden have already started to install tracks for charging at loading docks to eliminate tripping hazards and reduce the risk that drivers forget to connect the charging cable at each stop. The need to reinforce power grids also decreases, as a significant share of vehicles will be charged via electric roads. The number of chargers that will need to be installed will also go down dramatically.

Electric trucks will need an even higher capacity for charging than cars, and without the development of electric roads, the transformation of truck fleets to electric power is likely to require even bigger investments

---

4 In Europe, a large share of cars is fueled with diesel.

in superchargers and electricity grids than the change to electric cars.

It is unlikely that governments in all countries in the EU will be able to make the necessary investments over the next decade to prepare for a situation in 2035 when bans on sales of new fossil-fuel cars take effect. More about this later.

The example of the decision-making around electro-mobility is only one example of the hyperthink that is going on among decision-makers and experts in different areas. The idea that the market forces will be able to manage all kinds of development and change processes with minimum involvement in strategy development and planning is an example of mass confusion, and the lack of awareness of the requirements to implement these changes poses dangers to countries and to modern society at large.

A Need for a Dramatic Restructuring

What most people have not realized is that the rapid development and implementation of technology in the past decades has focused on technologies whose development, in many cases, started more than one hundred years ago, and in some cases, sixty or seventy years ago.

Now, these technologies have arrived at a level of maturity where their further development and application are likely to generate fewer advances in terms of cost reduction and increased value. And the technologies that experts, politicians, and citizens expect to drive economic growth in the coming decades are in the early stages of development. In contrast to the situation before and after the Second World War, the number of technologies at various stages of completion and maturity is much larger, and the number of areas in which the technologies can be applied is larger as well.

In this type of situation, it is not obvious which developments need to be supported to drive each technology to maturity. Government support for technology development and implementation is still necessary, but it is many times more difficult and demands more resources to figure out which strands of development should be supported, and which ought to be given less focus. The opportunities are so numerous that not all initiatives can be driven forward at top speed.

When computers were first developed, there was one programming language, Assembler, and a small number of application areas. With the early generations of computers, great developments were made in projects financed by the United States Department of Defense or branches of the armed forces that needed increased calculation power to develop advanced weapons systems.

The development of internet communication began in projects leading to the development of the ARPANET (the US Advanced Research Projects Agency Network), which connected US universities and research centers in the

1970s. Much later, ICT has become what economists call a set of *general-purpose technologies.* Other examples of such technologies are electricity, the combustion engine, and many others that are now part of everyday life. In 2023, there are literally millions of applications for computers and a vast number of different tools.

It is not as if governments have stopped supporting technology development. Financing continues in areas that have received financing in the past, but there is no strategy behind this funding that can lead to new breakthroughs. Technology development results in the creation of an increasing number of initiatives, but emerging technologies seldom receive the funding needed to take the leaps of development necessary for them to reach maturity. Funding is seldom based on an overall plan for development like those present in the case of the Apollo program, the development of computers, or the ARPANET.

The conversion of transport systems to electric vehicles is a case in point, but there are many other examples where ambitious goals are not matched by sufficient financing.

Instead of banning sales of gasoline and diesel cars from 2035, it is possible that this measure can realistically be taken later, due to the large investment that will be needed to make the transformation possible. The change to electric vehicles will become necessary because electricity is the only fuel that can replace gasoline and diesel on a large scale, but banning petroleum-fueled cars cannot be done until infrastructures have been expanded to make charging a large share of all vehicles possible. In most countries, this is likely to take more than one decade.

Formidable Challenges

A few additional figures indicate that countries face more formidable development challenges than previously realized. In the case of autonomous vehicles, a large capacity for computing, data storage, and communication will be needed. It may seem as if car makers, in particular Tesla, are on their way to mastering autonomy. The most advanced vehicles are currently at Level 2 in development, with Level 5 representing fully autonomous vehicles. Most vehicles at present have no autonomous functionalities at all, an important fact to keep in mind.

Level 2 means that cars can travel on motorways, changing lanes and overtaking other vehicles, but the driver needs to be ready at all times to take over control.

One of the main challenges of autonomous vehicles is the vast amount of data generated by cameras and radars as they move through traffic. According to Siemens, the amount of data generated is so extreme that one thousand fully autonomous vehicles would generate nineteen petabytes (19,000 terabytes) of data for every hour of driving. It takes all two billion daily users of Facebook almost five days to generate the same amount of information.[5]

5   https://blogs.sw.siemens.com/thought-leadership/2019/11/14/the-data-deluge-what-do-we-do-with-the-data-generated-by-avs/.

A large share of the data generated will have to be processed in each vehicle, to reduce latency and reduce the risk of incidents due to delayed decisions. In 2021, Facebook ran eighteen campuses of a total of eighty-five buildings containing more than one hundred thousand servers, to make it possible for users to store and process data. To make the use of autonomous vehicles possible on a large scale, a vast amount of computing capacity will have to be compressed to fit inside a few computer chips in a vehicle. In addition to the need to greatly expand the storage capacity of a computer chip, a substantial amount of that data will have to be communicated to servers in data centers. Large amounts of data must be processed by computers that will control traffic flows consisting of tens of thousands or hundreds of thousands of autonomous vehicles.

Moore's Law captures the growth of processing capacity, stating that the number of transistors that can be fitted on a certain area of a computer chip doubles every twenty-four months. At present one hundred thousand transistors can be fitted on an area the diameter of a human hair. Computer chips are made through *growing* semiconductors almost on an atom-by-atom, or molecule-by-molecule, basis. The semiconductor industry is fast approaching the limits of what is physically possible. To, over the next decade or two, compress information and create the communication and computing power needed for large numbers of autonomous vehicles is likely to require leaps in the development of chips and communication technology that surpasses Moore's Law, which has correlated well with the actual speed of development since 1965.

Extreme Challenges — Archaic Approach

The challenges are vast, and the number of areas of technology development that need to be supported to fulfill the promises of present-day technology optimists is growing. Countries and companies need to approach these challenges in a new way. An overall view must be taken of the challenges, existing financing strategies need to be reviewed, and new strategies will become necessary.

Regardless of the philosophy applied up until now, decision-makers need to understand that technology development requires large-scale and long-term government financing to tackle the most important technical issues and build the first generations of systems that will be required to conquer the future.

Governments are the only entities that have the incentive and resources to take such an overview of the development challenges, and the governments with access to the largest amounts of resources available for development are those of the United States, the EU, and a small number of other countries. The countries of the EU enjoy the advantage of being able to develop an overall strategy and then divide roles and tasks between them based on that strategy. The United States has a long-standing record of tackling large-scale challenges by mobilizing its resources to solve the most pressing technical issues. However, while the US government started the development of space travel, computers, the internet, nuclear power, and a host of other technologies and financed innovation and implementation for decades, the EU has so far not used its significant joint resources to tackle large-scale development challenges in a systematic way.

In preparing for the future, hyperthink is at play. Governments plan to achieve what is almost impossible, in a number of areas in parallel, without planning and without dedicating the financing necessary to achieve those ambitious goals. It is not likely that they will succeed. In reality, the approach based on hyperthink is putting the affluence of our present society at peril and creates a huge risk for future generations that the future will be neither as comfortable, nor supported by as advanced technologies as many presently believe.

2

How Did We End Up Here?

Large amounts of resources will be needed to make great development leaps. At present, resources are spread ever thinner across an increasing number of technology areas. Important initiatives cannot succeed unless they receive enough funding for technologies to rapidly reach maturity.

Governments need to map the landscape of innovation and technology development, identify the most important initiatives, and drive development in these areas forward. Public investment reduces the risk for private investors and opens opportunities that can speed up development even further.

The landscape of innovation is growing increasingly complex. Few have a realistic picture of how the future so many are taking for granted can be created.

The Future Similar to the Past?

Most people seem to believe that the future is going to be similar to the past, only much, much better. Technical development will continue, and the promises of services based on artificial intelligence, autonomous vehicles, a resource-efficient and clean economy, and nuclear fusion will be fulfilled within the lifetimes of the present or the next generation.

According to this way of viewing the world, resources in terms of manpower, energy, data storage capacity, or money are not likely to present problems. Regardless of how many development and implementation programs are pursued in parallel, all or most are likely to succeed. Regardless of how many man-hours or trillion dollars of investment will be needed to go through with them, all can become reality.

Intelligent people subscribe to this view of development likely because nobody has questioned it. So far, few people seem to have realized that economic growth and technical development by design lead to increasing complexity in society, complexity being defined as the number of different tools that are used in society at a particular time.[6]

---

6 Complex societies were analysed and described by the archaeology professor Joseph Tainter in his book *The Collapse of Complex Societies*. Tainter argued that increasing complexity is the reason behind the collapse of societies in the past, such as the Roman Empire, the Maya, Inca, and many more. Before Tainter's book, a number of different explanations of collapse had been used, but Tainter argued that all of the societies he had analysed had managed to cope with challenges in the past that were similar to the ones that brought them down. Tainter claimed that a higher level of complexity was the reason why these societies could not handle the challenges that lead to their downfall. The definition of complexity, according to Tainter, is a higher degree of specialisation in society, and one way to measure the degree of complexity of a society is by counting the number of different tools that are used by different specialists.

The rapidly increasing number of ICT tools that have been developed since the first computer was invented provides an illustration of this. By 2023, the number of computer-based tools has grown into the hundreds of thousands, possibly millions.

Similar developments have been going on in other areas as well. One hundred years ago there were a few qualities of steel. Now, there are thousands of qualities, including alloys with other metals and minerals that provide particular properties (for example heat or acid resistance), or suitability for different purposes. There are also qualities of steel that are manufactured using lower resource-consuming production methods and ones that have been made using hydrogen as the primary energy carrier, delivering fossil-fuel–free steel. In chemicals, a similar development is going on, creating tens of thousands of chemicals with different properties. In plastics, there are hundreds of varieties of plastics with properties suitable for specific purposes. While these developments are in many ways impressive, complexity adds cost to society and makes it more vulnerable.

Development constantly generates new ideas for materials, products, and machinery, and each product can often be further developed into different varieties. The more innovation, the more development projects will be pursued and financed, spreading resources thin across many areas. There is the apparent risk that no area will get enough resources to successfully bring to fruition programs that will be critical for the future of society.

Spreading resources thinly across an increasing number of specialized areas is likely to slow down development, rather than the opposite.

It should be clear that at some point the variety of new and important projects will be so great that they cannot all be pursued in parallel. Many development programs can be started that may lead to the development of a prototype or a beta version of a computer application. After all, it only takes so many engineering hours to develop a prototype of a computer program or, for example, an electric car. A few electric car companies can be started around the world that sell increasingly large numbers of electric cars, making it seem as if the development of electromobility is unstoppable with no need to plan or manage the transformation.

But, if we take a closer look, it will require very large amounts of resources, in terms of money, manpower, and production capacity, to expand global power production by some 50 percent to make it possible for every person on the planet to drive an electric car. Not to mention all the other activities that will be needed to implement electromobility on a large scale, such as changes to the auto, fuel, and utilities industries. In addition to these changes, a new industry for electromobility services must be developed.

The resources that will be needed to drive the conversion from the present small share of electric vehicles to a complete replacement of petroleum-fueled cars, buses, and trucks will be ten, twenty, or perhaps one hundred times larger than the resources that have been necessary to drive the development through its early phases.

So far, very few people have considered the amounts of resources needed to change transport systems to electric propulsion let alone started to add up the amounts that will become necessary to drive that development forward in parallel with a number of other large-scale changes.

Abstract and Counterproductive

Understanding this way of reasoning is not so difficult when it is explained in an accessible way, but few people have an incentive to pursue these thoughts to their logical conclusion.

A person who is offered a job in the automotive industry with the task of participating in the development of the next generation of electric cars is not likely to start to consider the resources required to convert all vehicles in the world to electric drive.

The same is true for employees in other industries. Each specialist area of development is like a silo where thousands of people work to bring about the next generation of technologies. Development in each area is very resource-demanding, and the different teams are not likely to take the time and money needed to map the landscape of development silos.

In the same way, it does not seem to have occurred to decision-makers that it will be important to explore the entire landscape of initiatives to get a picture of the growing complexity of our human society or analyze the challenges of driving a rapidly increasing number of development projects to fruition. The decision to ban the sales of new gasoline and diesel cars and subsidize car purchases and installation of chargers is not likely to lead to the development of cost-effective systems for electromobility.

Instead, researchers, engineers, experts, and employees that work in each of their respective silos are more likely to promote their area of development as a critical challenge for mankind to master.

People, in general, are likely to believe that before politicians made the decision to ban the sales of new gasoline and diesel cars, someone must have observed this complexity and made sure that it will be possible.

Adding up the resources needed would be a very abstract task for most people, and many are bound to think that it is impossible. While it is impossible to add them up precisely, it is possible to get a rough picture of the resources and activities required and make an estimate of whether it will be feasible to go through with the transformation of car fleets in only three decades at the same time as rapidly expanding fleets of electric trucks and buses.

It will also be possible, and necessary, to map the

development landscape and start to count the number of silos of development that are growing and compare the amounts of resources available with the amount that would be necessary to succeed with all the development efforts that have been, and are about to be, started.

When leaders, experts, and people, in general, discuss these things, the aspects of prioritization and financing of entire cycles of development need to be discussed more often.

It is possible to estimate resource needs and make realistic plans for entire innovation programs. After all, President Kennedy must have had some estimate of the resources needed to send a man to the moon in nine years' time and bring him safely back to Earth. The Apollo program "only" involved the building of a small number of rockets, a few moon landers and space capsules, a launch ramp, a control center, and a few other paraphernalia.

The global change from petroleum-fueled to electric transportation will require the construction of two or three hundred nuclear reactors or the equivalent with a total capacity amounting to perhaps 50 percent of the presently installed generation capacity across the world. Parts of all the power grids in all large towns and cities are likely to need reinforcement, and more than one billion gasoline and diesel vehicles need to become replaced by electric varieties, only to mention a few of the most obvious aspects of the change.

Hyperthink — A Type of Fast "Groupthink" Based on Mass Confusion

In his classic book *Thinking, Fast and Slow*, Professor Daniel Kahneman relates the ground-breaking research he and his colleague Amos Tversky did on decision theory. After decades of research, they concluded that people have two systems for problem-solving and decision-making: System 1 and System 2. System 1 is the system we use when we make everyday decisions about things that we are familiar with. System 2 is used when we take the time to consider facts and carefully reason toward a conclusion.

One example of a problem they posed to thousands of students at American universities was formulated as follows:

"Linda is thirty-one years old, single, outspoken, and very bright. She majored in philosophy. As a student she was deeply concerned with issues of discrimination and social justice, and also participated in antinuclear demonstrations."

The researchers asked which of the following alternatives was the most probable: "Linda is a bank teller," or "Linda is a bank teller and is active in the feminist movement." Contrary to logic, between 83 and 90 percent of students at major universities chose the second alternative. The logical fallacy is apparent as the number of bank tellers is larger than the number of feminist bank tellers, so the probability of Linda being a bank teller will inevitably be higher than that of her being a feminist bank teller. When students were given the opportunity to explain why they chose the second alternative, one of them replied that he or she thought the researchers were only asking for their opinion.[7]

In this and other cases studied, subjects had access to information that they did not use while making their decisions. Instead of considering all the relevant facts, they settled for the answer that first came to mind, which was often the wrong one.

The researchers concluded that the use of System 1, the system geared toward fast thinking, often leads subjects to jump to conclusions and make incorrect decisions. In many cases we would be advised to use System 2 instead, the system we use for deliberate reasoning, taking all facts into consideration.

Another type of phenomenon that leads people to leave their better judgment behind, has been labeled *groupthink*. This happens when decision-makers belong to groups of like-minded individuals, where the similar backgrounds and training of the individuals lead them to perceive a situation in a similar way and not consider the complete range of alternatives.

The author of the book *Groupthink*, Christopher Booker, defines his subject in the following way in the summary of the book:

"The adoption of a common view or belief not based

7   The example was described on pp 156-159 of *Thinking, Fast and Slow*, by Daniel Kahneman.

on objective reality; the establishment of a consensus of right-minded people, an 'in group'; and the need to treat the views of anyone who questions the belief as wholly unacceptable. He shows how various interest groups, journalists, and even governments in the twenty-first century have subscribed to this way of thinking, with deeply disturbing results."

Booker describes several situations throughout history when entire generations have become subject to group-think and made decisions that have been catastrophic for leaders. He describes, for example, the events that led to the French Revolution as a process of groupthink, and he examines the development of political correctness since the 1960s and draws a similar conclusion.

The researcher who coined the phrase, Yale psychologist Dr. Irving Janis, concluded that the decisions that led up to the US invasion of the Bay of Pigs in 1961, when the Kennedy administration decided to invade Cuba, were based on groupthink. The invasion was a failure, and it does not seem to have occurred to President Kennedy and his closest aides that the Cuban army would be able to stop an invasion by the United States.

In this type of situation, the members of the administration had access to information about the strength of the Cuban forces and the terrain surrounding the Bay of Pigs, but they failed to use it. They also failed to ask critical questions. It would perhaps have been possible to anticipate the failure, but the decision-makers did not.

Bigger than Groupthink — Hyperthink?

In the present situation, experts and decision-makers have failed to analyze the complexity and magnitude of a number of challenges of the future. This seems to be a cognitive failure on another level. In the debate about electromobility and autonomous vehicles, the transformation to a sustainable society, which includes the development of a resource-efficient, often referred to as *circular,* economy, is taken to be unproblematic. Neither the process nor the activities nor the financing are discussed.

Now, as governments have started to make decisions to transform key parts of the economy to sustainable systems and many experts are arguing that more resources need to be invested in the activities of the transformation, we, as a society, have no understanding of the scale and complexity of the development that lies ahead of us. Entire territories of ignorance have developed, and political correctness keeps people from asking pertinent questions like the ones posed in this book.

The terrain of development silos and the territories of ignorance that surround them need to be explored. Experts have not started to map in detail the resources and activities that will be needed to successfully transform the world to sustainability, implement autonomous vehicles, or go through with the other large-scale changes on the horizon.

Instead, funding has been provided for research and

development efforts on a small scale. Now that we can start to calculate the amount of development that will be needed, we realize that each of the changes envisioned is likely to require more resources and investment than any other transformation or development program of the past.

One of the main differences between the transformations discussed in this book and previous examples of the development of computers, aviation technologies, the internet, and most other developments of the past, is that few developments of the past were driven against a pressing timeline. Perhaps, the need to change the world to sustainability should have led decision-makers to ask questions about the resource needs and start projects with the aim of developing realistic plans and timelines.

On the other hand, high-profile experts and activists like David Attenborough, Greta Thunberg, and Al Gore have repeatedly stated that it will be possible to reduce emissions of carbon dioxide and go through with other changes necessary in time to halt climate change, if only governments dedicate more resources to the transformation. There are many experts on sustainability that also pose as experts on the timeline of the necessary changes, even though few researchers or experts have even started to explore the resources that will be necessary to drive these changes toward success.

In his 2021 book, *How to Avoid a Climate Disaster*, Bill Gates argues that countries will have to double or triple power production to create a sustainable society. Despite this statement by a prominent expert and former business leader, little effort has been made to investigate these needs and start to prepare for the expansion. Gates himself does not describe how the transformation program should be organized, financed, or managed.

When we look at Gates' estimate of the required resources, it appears as if the goal to achieve the change over the coming decades is unlikely to be met without developing a strategy and a plan. To succeed, governments must prioritize the most important changes and identify the activities and investments that will be necessary to realize those ambitious goals. They then need to make plans to ensure all preparations are made in a timely fashion.

I suggest the term hyperthink to describe the phenomenon of high ambition with no corresponding plan. Hyperthink poses a threat to our entire civilization. It stops leaders and people in general from making realistic plans for the development of the future. It leads us to make very risky and foolhardy decisions while at the same time convincing each other that all is well and that development has never made more rapid progress than at present.

It is likely that the opposite is true. Rapid development has been going on based on technologies that have become mature in recent decades. In the case of the technologies and business models necessary to build the future, innovation is going on in more areas than ever before, but there are not enough resources invested in any area to drive development forward at the pace necessary to make the breakthrough innovations and large-scale implementations of new technologies that people expect.

Why Our Brains Believe in False Information

Psychologists confirm that human brains are wired to believe in false information. The more familiar the information seems and the more often it gets repeated, the more likely it is that we will believe it.

In his November 3, 2022, *Washington Post* article, Richard Sima quotes prominent psychologists who describe the problem from different angles:

- Nathan Walter, professor of communication studies at Northwestern University: "On every level, I think that misinformation has the upper hand."
- Stephan Lewandowski, a cognitive psychologist at the University of Bristol: "By default, people will believe anything they see or hear. That makes a lot of sense because most things we're exposed to are true."
- Nadia Brashier, professor at Purdue University: "So, if you hear something over and over again, probabilistically, it's going to be the true thing."[8]

---

8   https://www.washingtonpost.com/wellness/2022/11/03/misinformation-brain-beliefs/.

In the modern world, many false claims are repeated over and over again on social media and in books and articles. It is highly likely that people are going to believe them. Even though people today are better educated and more knowledgeable than people were in the past, we are not experts, at least not in most areas, and it is difficult to see through false information.

As an increasing number of people start to believe in falsehoods and bring them up in discussions, it becomes increasingly likely that other people are also going to believe them and pass them on in their turn.

And, according to those cited above, it is difficult to erase false information from the minds of people. The more the information has been repeated, the harder it becomes to erase it. Even if someone hears a true explanation, it becomes increasingly difficult to remember it. The false worldview becomes ingrained into a person's personality, and it becomes part of their identity.

For example, in people's minds, if something works on a small scale, why should it not also work on a large scale? Many are not likely to realize that though a city can easily accommodate the use of one thousand cars, it can still be problematic and require many years of planning to build up car fleets of ten or one hundred million cars on a continent.

Another example: If people see many foreigners who work in different positions in a country and many foreign products are sold in stores, they can easily draw the conclusion that the free movement of goods and labor makes it more difficult for local people and products to compete. It takes a conscious train of thought to realize that open markets contribute to economic growth and that competition strengthens the economy and creates more jobs, which benefits all in the long run.

Even if some jobs are taken by people from other countries, there will be more jobs for local workers to apply for, and even if some of the goods sold are made abroad, open markets will increase the business opportunities for local companies abroad and in the domestic market. In the end, research has confirmed that collaboration between countries in the EU and through free-trade agreements benefits all and that the problem of unemployment cannot be solved by exiting such collaborations, the way the UK did through Brexit.

When people start to believe in false information, the calm acceptance of people around them and the fact that not even the experts raise an alarm indicate that there is nothing to worry about. If not even the most prolific advocates of stronger sustainability measures argue that plans need to be made for the transformation, there must be no need for such plans.

Why would Bill Gates, Al Gore, or Elon Musk not warn of the scale and complexity of the change to sustainability? Surely, they must have a good enough understanding of the development lying ahead of us. They would have warned if there seemed to be any problems lurking.

Well, Elon Musk has expressed his conclusions, but only one hour into an interview at a conference on computer programming. Clearly, the value of Tesla may plummet if people realize that the change to electromobility may not be as unproblematic as experts indicate. Other experts may not have warned us because describing the complexity is not their focus. Each of them has other goals, and discussing these things may not help in their pursuit.

Bill Gates, for example, purports to show the way forward in his book. He may have considered it to be counterproductive to go into the intricacies of the change and describe the complexity or admit that he does not know how the conversion could be achieved.

Only a small number of people have the incentive to scrutinize development plans and identify obstacles. I am one of them.

Hyperthink — Groupthink in Entire Countries or in the Western World at Large

Hyperthink is a process by which leaders and experts inadvertently or deliberately use mass confusion to change the course of history and lead development into paths that potentially threaten the future of modern society.

Hyperthink is a type of superficial thinking in which not all relevant facts are taken into consideration. The difference between hyperthink and groupthink is that hyperthink involves groupthink in entire countries, or in the western world at large. According to this definition, the examples given by Christopher Booker in his book would be seen as examples of hyperthink.

The reason why I suggest that a new concept should be used is that the phenomenon of hyperthink poses a threat to our modern society in a way that is not the case when small government teams make ill-advised decisions, such as in the case of the Bay of Pigs Invasion.

Hyperthink is closely related to political correctness. Ideas that are not politically correct, such as the one suggesting that the large-scale conversion of transport systems to electromobility will require large-scale government financing and systematic management of the change process, are avoided by politicians, business leaders, and experts alike. As much as hyperthink involves unwarranted optimism about some aspects of development, it results in total blindness to others.

It is definitely politically correct to argue that more resources need to be invested in the transformation to a sustainable society, but it is not politically correct to discuss how the ambitious goals set for the change process can be achieved, unless you argue that the cost to society will be low and that the transformation can be achieved over the course of one or two decades. It is politically correct to argue that the use of autonomous vehicles can help reduce the need for everyone to own their own car, but it is not politically correct to ask if the time when it will be possible for many to use fully autonomous vehicles will lie in the far-off future.

What Is Mass Confusion?

Mass confusion is a mindset of large swathes of the population that leads them to falsely believe that a particular way forward would be possible and preferable, without having access to all relevant facts, or when some of the facts have been distorted to support a particular political agenda.

Mass confusion is often based on sound ideas, but the reasoning is not taken to its logical conclusion. Instead, leaders and experts tend to use hyperbolic statements that have been insufficiently explored, and that are not supported by facts, to build trust and support among large groups in society.

Mass confusion and hyperthink tend to create large blind areas that people are not allowed to enter in discussions or even in their private thoughts.

The Opposite of Hyperthink

Successful projects throughout history have been meticulously planned. Experts and project managers have gone into every detail, from the start, to identify all the activities that will be necessary to achieve the end result. Once they have identified the activities, they have estimated the number of resources needed to perform each activity.

We can use the Apollo program as an example. When President Kennedy challenged the nation to send a man to the moon and bring him safely back to Earth before the end of the decade, NASA started to meticulously plan all the aspects of the program that had to be taken care of.

In cases of hyperthink, no detailed planning is carried out and no organization or management team is given the responsibility for the overall result. In these cases, neither the total amount of resources needed is investigated, nor is the size of the necessary budget determined, and no overall budget is dedicated to the project. Only some aspects of projects may receive funding, such as the subsidies for electric cars and charging posts that are offered by European governments. Other critical aspects are neglected, such as the need to expand power production or the reinforcement of power grids needed.

The Root of the Problem

As it seems, this lack of analysis and planning is not based on any conscious decision by leaders or experts. Most times, the politicians, experts, and business leaders involved seem to genuinely believe in what they are saying.

Hyperthink seems to arise because the leaders of a movement have not analyzed all aspects of the issues and have no complete knowledge of the subject matter they discuss or work with. In the case of the change to a sustainable society, many activists and experts are biologists, ecologists, or experts in climate science. When they say that a reduction in emissions of carbon dioxide can be achieved in time to avoid a climate disaster, they are not likely to know how to analyze the complexity of the change processes needed or understand the amount of investment or the changes to industries that will become necessary.

People who work in big companies know that change programs in individual corporations, like General Electric or IBM, often take a decade or more, and to succeed need to be well managed and invested with large amounts of resources. Still, even such programs often fail, and companies may need to start and restart several times to achieve ambitious change goals. To change entire countries, or the whole global economy to sustainability, will be even more complex and demanding of resources. The probability of failure will be much higher than in the case of change programs driven in companies.

Sometimes, as in the case of the change to a sustainable society, there are few opponents, and there are no groups in society with a strong enough incentive to discuss the realism of proposals. In other cases, for example, Brexit, the arguments are abstract, and large groups of people want to believe that there is a very simple solution to the issues at hand. Usually, a large element of wishful thinking boosts mass confusion.

In fact, neither in the statement by the President of Toyota in December of 2020, when he argued that electromobility would require a very large investment in infrastructure, nor in the 10-point plan for sustainability launched by Boris Johnson's UK government at the same time, nor in the book *How to Avoid a Climate Disaster*, by Bill Gates, was the need for plans or managed transformation and development programs mentioned.

In the case of the change to a sustainable future, the one-sided focus on the environmental issues and the technical aspects of the transformation has created vast territories of ignorance. The symptoms and mechanisms seem to be similar to groupthink, but the process takes place on a global scale, and this results in numerous oversights created by hyperthink that threaten the future of our entire civilization.

3

My Own Path of Development

I have studied the challenges of large-scale technology development and implementation for more than twenty-five years. Now, an increasing number of leaders and technical experts have begun to realize that large investments will be needed to build the society of the future.

Many still believe that the change will be automatic, entirely driven by market forces. But market-driven development does not steer toward a specific goal. The fledgling systems of electromobility and the circular economy are not likely to become competitive against incumbent technologies without large-scale and long-term financing by governments.

A Long Journey

To understand how difficult it may be, even for people with a relevant background and a large interest in mapping the change to understand the process, it makes sense to relate some aspects of my own journey toward understanding. I started out in 2004, somewhat unwillingly.

The fact that I have focused on only a narrow set of issues can be contrasted with the situation facing politicians and business leaders who have to deal with a much broader range of topics. They will inevitably have less time to make sense of each subject and come to relevant conclusions. To an increasing extent, they become dependent on experts. Experts are likely to differ in their views, and it will still be up to decision-makers and administrators to form their own opinions and make decisions.

In 2004, I read *The Party's Over*, by Richard Heinberg, in which the starting point is the fact that oil is a finite resource and that at some point in the future, oil production will reach its peak, and from that time, it will decline. This, according to Heinberg and some other experts on oil production, will occur much sooner than people have previously thought. The book brought up a lot of facts about oil discovery and production, establishing, for example, that the largest volumes of oil were discovered in the 1960s and 1970s when prices were very low. Nowadays, when the price has gone up to almost one hundred dollars per barrel, very little new oil is found, despite the fact that ever larger sums of money are spent exploring.

The author argued that the peak in oil production would occur much earlier than oil companies would admit and that countries need to rapidly start to prepare for a future of declining oil production. The most important form of preparation would be to develop and implement new transport systems that use renewable fuels, for example, electricity.

I realized that the preparations to replace petro-leum-based transportation with transport systems using renewable fuels would have to start as soon as possible, because it would take many decades to go through with the change.

At that time in 2004, it was not clear which fuels would be the most suitable to replace oil. Sustainability experts promoted biofuels like ethanol, methanol, biogas, rapeseed oil, or black liquor (a by-product of paper pulp production). Electric propulsion was not high on the agenda at the time. Volkswagen and other car manufac-turers developed biogas cars. Regional governments in Sweden invested in biogas-fueled buses for public trans-portation, and a network of filling stations for natural gas with a share of biogas were built. Similar steps were taken to change car fleets to natural gas in combination with biogas, the latter being a mixture of methane and carbon dioxide produced through digestion of organic waste in an oxygen-free environment.

A large number of books and reports were written on biological fuels, mostly from a technical perspective. The texts recounted the advantages of each fuel, rather than discussing the resources that would be needed to go through with a transformation of the world's transport systems to one or several of these fuels.

I interviewed many companies involved in the change. One of them was Volvo Trucks, then the largest manufacturer of heavy trucks outside China. Volvo produces Volvo, Nissan, Renault, and Mack Trucks, all strong brands in the heavy truck market. In 2009, Volvo launched a series of seven prototype trucks with engines developed for the use of seven different biological fuels, or in some cases combinations of two different biofuels.

None of the prototypes included an electric engine. The title of the campaign was "With the Climate Issue in Focus" and the seven fuels were biodiesel, synthetic diesel, DME (dimethyl ether), methanol and ethanol, biogas, biogas in combination with biodiesel, and hydrogen in combination with biogas.

A few years later, Volvo Trucks set their sights entirely on electric drive, as auto industry experts became convinced of the possibility of running heavy trucks on 100 percent electricity.

My first book on the large-scale transformation to renewable fuels, *Global Energy Transformation*, was published by Palgrave in 2009. In it, I concluded that a large-scale transformation would have to be organized as a large-scale change program, similar to other transformation and development programs in history.

In the book, I discussed three such programs, the transformation of US industry to military production in 1942, the Marshall Plan, funded by the United States government, which helped European countries recover after the war, and the Apollo program, started by President Kennedy in 1961.

I concluded that the type of management structures and financial and control mechanisms that were applied in these programs would have to be used by governments to succeed with the transformation to transport systems based on renewable fuels. This change would be very different from the previous change programs. The future program would need a unique set of management mechanisms and governments would need to learn from the earlier examples.

In a later book I used the impressive feat by the Republic of Venice of constructing more than 450 ships and furnishing them with food and equipment for the 4,500 knights, 4,500 horses, and 20,000 foot soldiers of the Fourth Crusade in 1201 as a further example. It took 30,000 maritime specialists to sail and row the crusaders to their destination, half the adult population of Venice. To feed the army, each man needed 377 kilos of bread and flour, 200 kilos of cereals and beans, and 300 liters of wine annually.[9] The large-scale development Venice achieved

---

9 Crowley, Roger. *City of Fortune, How Venice Won and Lost a Naval Empire.* Faber and Faber, London 2011.

in only one year indicated that civilizations have achieved impressive goals of industrial development throughout history. At the time, the number of people in Venice was only 100,000, which makes it even more impressive.

In *Global Energy Transformation,* I also concluded, through a comparison between biofuels, hydrogen, and other alternatives, that electricity would be the only fuel that could be produced in large enough quantities and that it therefore would be the only option for the future.

A further advantage of electricity, compared to, for example, hydrogen, was that a large-scale infrastructure for the production and distribution of power is already in place. Large additional resources for power generation and distribution would have to be built and grids may have to be expanded, but the basic facilities are already in place and the expansion of fleets of electric vehicles could go on for several years awaiting the expansion measures. In the case of the expansion of hydrogen, no infrastructure for the large-scale production and distribution of the gas is in place. Such an infrastructure would need to be built almost from scratch and power production would have to be expanded even more dramatically than in the case of the change to battery-electric vehicles.

At this point I did not know how much electricity would be needed to fuel electric vehicles. No one had started to ask the question. One or two years later, in a report from Elforsk, a research project run by the Swedish institute for the research into electricity systems, it was stated that the power needed to fuel all Swedish cars amounted to only 10 TWh per year.

At the time, this corresponded to the annual production from two of Sweden's nuclear reactors. I calculated backward and found that some 4.5 million cars requiring 10 TWh in total would mean that each car needed about 2,500 kWh per year. With 15,000 km driven on average per year, at that time, it meant that an electric car needs 1.5 kWh to drive 10 km. This is a relevant estimate, although a bit conservative.

Around 2010 I calculated, for example, that the 260 million cars in Europe would need some 600 TWh of electricity annually, which at the time corresponded to more than one hundred nuclear reactors. Since then, the average production of upgraded reactors has gone up to 9 TWh and the average production of a new reactor amounts to 11 TWh, which means that the number of reactors needed has halved.

To me, the use of the unit of nuclear reactors has not been a way to promote nuclear power. The number of nuclear reactors is a more tangible measure than the power need expressed in TWh. Most people know that a nuclear reactor represents a significant investment, somewhere in the area of five or six billion dollars, and fifty or one hundred reactors would mean a very large investment and a program spanning several decades for its completion.

Since 2010, when I started making this type of calculation, Germany has built an impressive number of wind turbines, a total of thirty thousand land-based turbines. In 2021, they produced 100 TWh of electricity. This indicates that to supply all European cars with electricity would require the power generated by 150,000 wind turbines of the average capacity installed in Germany. This number of turbines would at least be sufficient in the summer, as long as there is enough wind.

These are calculations that I have been able to do in the last few years. From 2004 until my latest book, *The Blind Guardians of Ignorance*, published in December 2020, the interest in the transformation to electromobility was lukewarm, to say the least. Few organizations or governments published anything of interest on large-scale transformation, and few people took an interest in these matters. The EU had decided to make the union carbon neutral by 2050, which meant that only electric vehicles would be used by then, but very little attention was paid to the change process.

Then, in December 2020, a small number of people started to make decisions or publish statements:

- Boris Johnson's UK government launched a 10-point program for sustainability in which one of the items was to ban the sales of combustion engine cars from 2030. There was no mention of the fact that the change of all thirty-two million UK cars to electric drive would require some 65 TWh of electricity, 20 percent of the current UK production of 325 TWh per year. The plan also did not mention that more generation capacity would be needed in the coldest weeks of cold winters, or that the transformation of fleets of heavy vehicles would require additional amounts of power, as would some of the other points of the program, for example, the promotion of low-carbon hydrogen as an energy carrier.

- The president of Toyota, Akio Toyoda, stated in a press release that Toyota did not see electromobility as a way forward. He argued that "the silent majority of the auto industry worldwide is still doubtful of electric cars." He also quoted calculations made by Toyota indicating that it would require between 135 and 358 billion dollars in infrastructure investment for Japan to convert its entire vehicle fleets to electric drive, too high a cost for the country, Toyoda argued. He also warned that Japanese power is generated by burning coal and natural gas, activities that emit large amounts of carbon dioxide.[10]

- Even though Toyoda made these statements, the company invested heavily in the development of electric vehicle technologies. Toyota has also invested heavily in the development of hydrogen fuel cells. Driving vehicles on hydrogen will require twice as much electricity for hydrogen production compared to driving similar distances using battery-electric cars. Toyoda did not outline how he saw the future development of the auto industry if electric vehicles would not become the selected technology.

10 https://observer.com/2020/12/toyota-akio-toyoda-electric-vehicle-japan-transition/

- In *How to Avoid a Climate Disaster,* published in February of 2021, Bill Gates argues that countries will have to double or triple power production to develop a sustainable industry.
- Later, in the summer of 2022, the chief manufacturing officer of the automaker Stellantis (owner of Opel, Peugeot, Chevrolet, Fiat, Citroen, and a number of other car brands), Arnaud Deboef, warned that the ban on the sales of new gasoline and diesel cars by the EU from 2035 may cause the car industry to collapse. He warned that electric cars may by then not be inexpensive enough for the general car buyer to afford them and that many people will not be able to buy electric cars from the time of the ban. This could, according to Deboef, lead to a collapse of the auto industry.[11]

Since December 2020, I have published articles debating the overall need for resources to make the transformation to electric vehicle systems and a circular economy in Sweden's daily business newspaper, *Dagens Industri.* I have also had the opportunity to present on the change to electromobility at various seminars and workshops, often to university professors involved in electromobility or to representatives from utilities and automotive companies. In addition to these presentations, I have appeared in several international podcasts.

---

11   https://www.bloomberg.com/news/articles/2022-06-29/stellantis-warns-of-car-market-collapse-if-evs-don-t-get-cheaper

Exploration of Resource Efficiency

While writing *Global Energy Transformation* in 2008, it became clear to me that it would most likely take longer to change transport systems to sustainable fuels than experts and decision-makers expected. I concluded that efforts to reduce transportation and resource consumption through other means would become necessary as well. With decreasing volumes of oil being produced in the future, the continuous expansion of petroleum consumption could not go on forever. The buildup of resources would have to start immediately, because the large-scale systems that would be needed, such as electric transport systems, would take decades to build. At the time I had no suitable umbrella term available to describe all the efforts to reduce dependence on oil, including reduced use of plastics, increasing local production, and a number of other measures.

In 2016 I got the opportunity to analyze the development of business based on the sustainability principles captured under the umbrella of *the circular economy*. In a project co-financed by the regional authority of the Skåne region in southern Sweden, I had the opportunity to analyze the progress of the circular economy to identify the means to speed up this development.

The "circular economy" is an umbrella term that includes the concepts of local production, re-use, standardization and modularization, biological materials, the product as a service, the sharing economy, and a few others.

As I performed interviews with experts and companies that offered products and services within the different areas of the circular economy, I realized that the concepts represented the type of principles for resource-saving that I had been looking for.

What I also realized was that the development of the circular economy stood at an even earlier stage than the development of electromobility. The use of biological plastics, for example, is minuscule compared to the vast usage of petroleum-based plastics across the globe, and the number of biological materials available for plastics production is small as well. A very large investment would be needed to significantly reduce the amounts of fossil plastics used, and new large-scale production and distribution systems for the raw materials would have to be developed.

A similar situation exists for local production. At present, a very small share of the world's food and other products are made and distributed locally. Small producers and promoters of locally produced food and other products are facing multiple challenges. One is the efficiency of national and global production and distribution systems. A large part of the explanation behind the highly competitive prices of all kinds of products is large production volumes and large manufacturers that deliver enormous volumes of goods into the distribution centers of large retail chains.

With smaller local producers, not only would the production cost increase. The same would happen to the cost of logistics, both to transport products from producers to shops and also for the handling in stores of products from a multitude of small manufacturers.

To significantly increase the share of local products, many companies focusing on regional markets will be needed. In addition to production facilities, there is also a need for inexpensive packaging and labeling solutions suitable for small producers, local wholesalers with competitive logistics solutions, and retailers that can take supplies from local companies in a cost-effective way. In short, extensive and cost-effective *ecosystems* of local producers will be needed to develop supply chains and change the supply of products and services to a significant share of locally produced items.

Through the project I realized that, despite how the circular economy is presented in the literature, the development of circular production and distribution systems is at an early stage of development. A large number of businesses need to be developed that make up different parts of the manufacturing and distribution ecosystems that will be needed to create competitive circular economy systems. The challenges of doing this are enormous. Existing companies have strong incentives to defend their present businesses, and it will be very difficult for new companies to compete against systems to a large extent made up of global giants with very well-known brands.

Through a series of circular economy projects, I have experienced the difficulties of transforming existing production and distribution into circular systems. I developed the ideas put forward in the report written for Region Skåne in 2016 into a book with the title *Circular Business Models*, which was published by Palgrave in 2018. The conclusion is that the change to a circular economy is not likely to succeed in the absence of large government investment and strong management of the transformation process.

The Development of E-Business

My first attempt at forecasting the technology and business development of the future was made in the area of e-business. Together with my then colleague David Lundberg, I co-wrote one of the first books on e-business strategy, titled *The Transparent Market,* published in 1998.

David and I predicted the growth of the internet as a marketplace and as a medium for advanced business communication, and the development over the past twenty years has, to a large extent, turned out as we described it. This, however, has been an entirely different type of development compared to that of the circular economy and sustainable transport systems:

– In many industries, digital businesses, from a very

early point in their development, reduced costs compared to traditional forms of distribution and supply chain management. Circular business models in many cases cause the cost to increase, and cost savings may be achieved far into the development, when more advanced business ecosystems have developed that can improve the efficiency of circular operations.

– E-business operators could benefit from the efficiency and brand recognition of existing manufacturers, logistics companies, and other service providers. E-business offered a new and more cost-effective way of communicating with customers directly, organizing supply chains and sending information from customers throughout the chains to manufacturers or brand owners.

The development of the circular economy requires the development of entirely new supply chains, which to a large extent will consist of companies and products that do not at present exist. While electronic business has given rise to the development of many companies, many incumbents make up the core of e-business supply chains. Incumbents are likely to have to take important roles in the development of electromobility and the circular economy, but they will have to develop new products and supply chains, which will inevitably take decades from start to finish.

Autonomous Vehicles

More recently, I turned my attention to the challenges of autonomous vehicles. Going back a number of years, many people I have discussed electromobility with have argued that the vehicle fleets of the future will be smaller than today. This is because autonomous vehicles will make it possible for many people to use the same vehicle.

According to these visions of the future, an autonomous vehicle will pick up one passenger at five in the morning and drive them to work. The same vehicle will then pick up another person that needs to be driven to the airport. A third person may then get off his shift at work and be driven home. In between the transport of people, vehicles may be used for the transportation of goods. Everything could be done in well-managed transport systems that make optimal use of all resources.

This type of system would have several advantages compared to the present situation, in which many cars are used for an hour most days and sit for the rest of the day, waiting for their drivers at work, at train stations, or airports.

According to autonomous vehicle visionaries, self-driving vehicles will in a few years contribute to making transportation more cost-effective. Cars will no longer need drivers, which reduces cost, and the cost of each vehicle can be shared between many users. Even if autonomous vehicles will be more expensive than the present types of cars, buses, and trucks, the extra cost will be offset by the savings of several users being able to share the same vehicles. In the case of transport vehicles, the opportunity to get rid of the driver would reduce the cost of transportation by truck or bus, taxi rides, and sending packages, or it would at least compensate for the higher purchase price of the vehicle.

Not only visionaries seem to believe in this. Investors have driven the value of some start-up companies that develop autonomous vehicles through the roof. The optimism among the financing community has been so great that some of the start-ups have risen to the status of *unicorns,* start-up companies valued at more than one billion dollars. This in itself seems to be a speculation bubble and an example of hyperthink.

I have spent less time investigating the different aspects of autonomous vehicles than I have analyzing the challenges of electromobility and the development of a circular economy. Meetings with managers at Ericsson and other electronics companies have provided an understanding of the challenges related to the communication between vehicles and data centers. Over the past year, I have had the opportunity to look into semiconductor development and get a picture of the challenges related to developing the coming generations of chips.

The actual reasoning and the data have been presented earlier in the book.

My Conclusions

Since 2004, I have made progress from a general idea of the complexity and scale of the transformation to sustainability to a relatively detailed understanding of the challenges and the type of process that will be necessary. From the beginning, I believed that the development could not possibly be achieved without large-scale and long-term government financing and management of the process. A few years later, I found the book *Is War Necessary for Economic Growth?* by Vernon W. Ruttan, which underscores the need for various forms of program management and funding by governments. The development we have experienced so far has confirmed this need, but few leaders or experts have taken the slow progress up until now into account when making decisions.

Some of the necessary technologies existed in early versions already in 2004. For example, there were early versions of electric cars, but the vehicles and the early systems for electromobility have to be developed into fully fledged and highly competitive products and services. Offerings need to be delivered by highly competitive companies in advanced supply chains and company ecosystems.

Unfortunately, it is likely to take a very long time to develop both highly competitive offerings and strong companies that deliver them, as there is little financing available to cover the high cost of developing and implementing the new technologies and systems on a large scale. Based on technologies and products, entire systems for electromobility and the various concepts contained under the umbrella of the circular economy need to be developed. They also need to be expanded to replace existing solutions.

The development of even single new companies and business models usually takes decades, and there are many pitfalls on the way. The complete rebuilding of several very large industries with hundreds of thousands of companies worldwide will take a very long time and require strict management. In the absence of managed programs, the result of the process is unpredictable.

The limited insight into the dynamics of change indicates that society is tied up in hyperthink, but some individuals are starting to question whether it will be possible to succeed if countries apply the present model of development.

Still, few people have turned their attention to key issues, concerning, for example, how the programs need to be financed, organized, and managed, but an increasing number agree that progress is slower than what would be needed and that strategies need to be put in place to focus resources in the most highly prioritized areas. In the past two or three years, I have met with many sustain-ability-minded individuals who have started to question whether countries will be able to successfully transform transport systems in the timeframe suggested by the decisions by the EU and in California.

It is a truism that no one here gets out alive, but our society and the affluence that has been built up through a process spanning centuries deserve to survive. We cannot develop a sustainable society for our children and grand-children if the present generations continue to neglect some of the most basic principles of technology and economic development.

Even if the goal would not be to create a sustainable society, a number of new technologies need to be developed rapidly to build a platform for economic growth over the coming decades. These technologies will need to be built in the way that technology development in the post-war era built the platform for the economic growth that the present generations have been enjoying the fruits of ever since.

We need to develop a sustainable society, but not at the expense of putting prosperity and affluence at risk in the process.

4

Territories of Ignorance

Hyperthink has made all kinds of people, from top leaders to ordinary citizens, blind to the most important aspects of the change to sustainability and technology development at large.

Successful development of new technologies requires managed development programs, large-scale government financing, and the creation of companies and organizations that are structured specifically to perform the different tasks needed to drive development forward.

With a tight time-schedule—like in the case of the Apollo program—very strict organization and management of the process will be needed.

Hyperthink – the Seed of Ignorance

Hyperthink, like groupthink, thrives in an atmosphere where people avoid discussing certain topics. Subjects that do not fit the correct worldview are deemed "politically incorrect," and around them huge territories of ignorance develop. In this type of environment, it becomes increasingly dangerous for individuals to put forward ideas that do not resonate well with the views that are accepted in society.

We can identify three tenets that are fiercely guarded by leading proponents of the faiths:

- Market-driven growth, exclusively
- No important risks arise
- Sustainability focus in the transformation

In each of these, many issues are suppressed, and the resulting discourse makes it impossible to elaborate on the topics and integrate key aspects of development into the debate. For this reason, subjects that should be viewed in combination to create a holistic picture are treated separately, as if they had nothing to do with each other.

As an example, in the government administrations of many countries, the ministry and authority responsible for environmental issues handles the transformation to sustainability. They work mainly with the reduction of emissions and the initiation of small-scale projects and activities aimed at creating circular systems. The ministry and authority responsible for industrial development, on the other hand, strives to create and maintain economic growth with a focus on making the companies of a country more competitive in global markets.

The attempts to reduce emissions and the use of resources by environmental agencies are usually of a small scale compared to the resources used and the emissions caused by the growth of the global economy. Little dialogue is going on about how the country's production processes can be transformed to sustainability on a large scale or how the goals of the Kyoto Protocol and other international agreements can be complemented by activities of industry that may bring about a truly sustainable system. For a society to be sustainable, transport systems need to be fully electric and production and distribution in most large industries need to be organized along circular, or sustainable, principles. A large share of production needs to be done using renewable materials. There is also no discussion of the investment that will be needed to build sustainable production and distribution systems along the lines of the circular economy.

Even if people do not see reduced emissions as the most critical goal, global oil production will reach its peak and go into decline. The production of shale oil and other forms of unconventional oil is not likely to grow to take over the bulk of oil production. For this reason, humanity needs to rapidly develop transport systems that can be fueled by electricity and, for example, find replacements for oil-based plastics.

While most politicians and business leaders agree that countries need to reduce emissions of carbon dioxide, the complete picture of the challenges and all the mitigation activities that will be needed are not discussed. Clearly, many things need to change, but it needs to be said frequently that all of this cannot be done at the same time, and not in a haphazard manner.

While the EU has set the goal of making the union carbon neutral by 2050, and a decision has been made to ban the sales of new gasoline and diesel cars from 2035, this has not yet led to the realization that achieving carbon neutrality will involve the reorganization of industry into more resource effective supply chains and distribution systems. The process of healing discourses and patterns of thought will be difficult, and it will take a long time.

Countries cannot create a sustainable society at the expense of affluence and financial prosperity. It can only be through economic growth and profitable companies that countries will be able to invest in the development of a sustainable society. It is time to acknowledge that the pursuit of differing goals requires that some goals and ideas will have to give way. The process of change will have to be set on a realistic timeline, and the methods used to drive the process must be adapted to the challenges at hand.

The following sections provide an overview of some of the more obvious areas of ignorance.

Forbidden Territory 1: Market-Driven Growth, Exclusively

Market-driven growth has become a paradigm that cannot be questioned. In our present economic system, growth and growth expectations play key roles. This is not primarily because the present generations in western countries demand more affluence, but because growth expectations maintain the value of resources and *maintain* and increase the prosperity of developed countries.

Ultimately, it is the increasing affluence of developed countries that spills over and helps poor countries rise out of poverty. Without growth expectations, the demand for shares in the stock market would dwindle, the willingness of investors to invest would be reduced, and consumption would decrease. This would create a vicious circle that would increase unemployment, reduce consumption, and make all countries poorer. In this type of situation, there will be fewer resources available to finance the change.

While these are facts related to the present economic system, the elaboration of these ideas becomes impossible because economic discourse is dictated by economists and politicians from all parts of the political spectrum who do not have the incentive to constructively discuss these matters, neither amongst themselves nor in public. Thus, the hegemony of the market in all areas becomes unquestioned, and all debaters who want to be taken seriously must first acknowledge this as a fact.

The market mechanisms are clearly the most efficient tools for allocating resources in mature markets, but as we have seen in the earlier chapters and will see in the chapters to come, government financing and development programs have played important roles in the development and implementation of technologies in the past. At present the EU, for example, finances projects in the early stages of development, and very large sums of money are spent to support innovation.

In many areas, once prototypes and early system solutions have been developed, companies and organizations end up in a situation often called the "valley of death," in which little or no funding is available to take technologies to large-scale deployment.

This leads to a situation where new technologies and prototypes are developed, but too few of these succeed in finding pilot customers. Among the companies that start to grow, many fail to embark on a path of sustainable growth. While this, to an extent, is the way the market works, it is important for society that we reach the goals of electromobility, a circular economy, and other prioritized developments. Companies that have developed technologies necessary for the transformations must survive and thrive.

In the Apollo program, NASA made sure that key assignments were placed with companies that had the financial capacity to perform the projects assigned to them and to develop and co-finance the activities they took part in. NASA not only built the resources to plan and monitor the technical development but also took the responsibility to nurture the space industry and make it grow.

The model that was used in many European countries in the past was based on public-private partnerships. Government agencies and publicly owned companies teamed up with leading companies to build railroads, electricity grids, phone networks, and many other large-scale and potentially risky innovation programs. These types of programs have been necessary, not only to build up the systems, but also to develop strong supply chains for the various products and services that are needed to build, operate, and maintain the systems through the early decades of their existence.

Governments financed these programs and ran the associated systems for many years until the technologies matured and the systems and their operation were, to a large extent, privatized. At present, it is expected that the market will do the financing and that private investors will take the entire risk both for technology development and for the development of large-scale systems.

In the United States, the government financed the development of various technologies, for example, computers and the internet. Ruttan drew the conclusion that long-term and large-scale government financing significantly sped up the development and implementation of these technologies and systems.

It is unlikely that present generations would have had access to ubiquitous computing power and internet-based communication without these investments. Maybe these resources would have been developed later, or not at all, without that financing. We cannot know for sure.

One of the areas where many expect market-driven development to build fully fledged and highly competitive systems is the area of charging infrastructure for electric vehicles. So far, investment in chargers has, to a large extent, been financed by public subsidies, at least in Europe. Tesla has developed a business model to finance the expansion of an extensive network of fast chargers, but other electric vehicle companies either lack the volumes or the premium-priced vehicles to make this possible.

For operators of charging infrastructure, it may be difficult to build profitable systems that cover entire countries. To make it possible for vehicle owners to drive everywhere, a sufficient number of chargers will be needed to charge all vehicles whenever needed. The need for redundancy will remain, as there must always be a charger available for the next customer. Unlike in many other markets, queues are unacceptable, at least queues in which drivers need to wait for half an hour or an hour every time they need to charge. This would dramatically reduce the efficiency, convenience, and pleasurability of driving.

One example of a place with seasonal needs is the Swedish ski resort of Sälen. It is located 110 miles from the larger towns of Falun and Borlänge. There are only a few hundred inhabitants in Sälen, but in the winter some one hundred and thirty thousand guests visit each week to ski and participate in other winter sports. Many come there by car, and supplies need to be delivered every week by truck. In a future with a large share of electric vehicles, all visiting cars and trucks will need to be charged there to be able to go back home. A similar situation exists at other seasonal tourist destinations.

The EU and national governments have provided generous financing plans to speed up the development of charging infrastructure. We all hope that the market will be able to finance the expansion from a point not too far into the future, but this is uncertain. Now, as some European countries are embarking on the expansion of electric truck fleets, the Swedish government, for example, has launched a program that finances 100 percent of the cost of the first fast chargers for trucks along major roads. While this may be necessary to get the process of building electric truck fleets going, it indicates that the need for public financing of the change to electric vehicles may be very large.

In an article published in November 2022, reporting the results of a study made on behalf of the European Automobile Manufacturer's Association (ACEA), the global management consulting firm McKinsey & Co concluded that to meet even the most conservative scenario of expansion of electric vehicles, European countries must increase the number of public charging posts installed every week from the present 1,600 to more than 10,000 in 2030. Utilities will also have to expand the capacity of power grids to facilitate the amount of charging needed.[12]

This type of expansion will represent a very big investment and a significant risk in case the goals for the expansion of electric vehicle fleets are not met. As already mentioned, an alternative to building stationary charging infrastructure will be the building of electric road networks. The process of financing programs, receiving planning permission, and planning the expansion will take several years, and large-scale projects need to start immediately for any significant networks of electric roads to be completed by 2035.

In the Apollo program, NASA managed a similar, albeit smaller and less complex challenge. The program did not involve the tricky task of building well-functioning markets for the new technologies, and it did not involve the development of a set of operators of infrastructure and services that had to become prosperous and profitable. NASA simply procured development services and the equipment needed to go to the moon. The development of markets for space technologies and services was developed much later, as the innovations became less expensive to use for market-based applications.

---

12 https://www.mckinsey.com/industries/automotive-and-assembly/our-insights/eu-ropes-ev-opportunity-and-the-charging-infrastructure-needed-to-meet-it.

To Make the World a Better Place

One example of a failed private investment that illustrates the financial risk involved comes from the company Better Place, founded in California in 2007. At the time electric cars only had batteries with a range of some 70 miles. The idea developed by the founder of Better Place, Shai Agassi, was to build battery-switching stations along major roads where drivers could switch to a fully charged battery. The goal of Better Place was to become the company that revolutionized electromobility and took electric vehicle charging systems from a novelty to a mass-market service.

The founders managed to get 850 million dollars in financing for the venture. The first country where the company built a complete network of switching stations was Denmark. This country was selected because they have high taxes on gasoline and diesel cars, it is a small country with the opportunity to build a relatively small number of switching stations to provide subscribers with the opportunity of traveling the whole country, and the government was prepared to make electric cars tax free.

Better Place built nineteen switching stations, but before the network was inaugurated in 2013, the company went bankrupt. At the time, Better Place received positive press in Denmark, but only a small number of customers signed up when the services were launched.

The example illustrates the immense risk necessary

for companies that want to build infrastructure for new transport technologies. To reduce the risk of investing, governments are likely to have to ensure that the technologies chosen will be used for the longer term, as was the case with the implementation of railways, electricity systems, phone systems, mobile phone systems, and several other developments of the past, and they are likely to have to contribute a significant portion of the funding, to reduce risk in the expansion of electromobility.

Forbidden Territory 2: No Important Risks Arise

The power supply and transportation are key areas in our modern society. Countries are dependent on the regular supply of electricity and the functioning of transport systems. Still, governments experiment in both of these areas without any plans that will ensure a secure power supply, reasonable price levels, or a controlled transformation to electric vehicles over the coming decades.

In the area of the power supply, governments make plans and decisions to drive development programs that will dramatically increase the demand for electricity. The change to electric vehicles is an area where the need for power has been grossly underestimated, but there are other areas of development that will also require significant amounts of electricity.

A large-scale conversion to hydrogen-fueled production plants or transportation will require large amounts of electricity. In northern Sweden, there are two projects to create fossil-free steel production. One is a greenfield investment in a new hydrogen-fueled steel plant, and the other is a brownfield conversion of an existing plant, owned by the steel company SSAB. Hydrogen production for these two plants may require as much as 50 TWh of electricity per year. The total Swedish production at present is 150 TWh.

There are plans to convert coastal shipping to electric or hydrogen-fueled ships. Initiatives are also being taken to develop electric or hydrogen-fueled airplanes. Both of these developments are in the early stages, but there are ambitious plans.

There are also plans in many countries to electrify industry. Many companies at present use fossil fuels like natural gas or coal to fuel their processes. Plans to convert the power supply to electricity will substantially increase the demand for power.

An increasing need for power also comes from other areas, such as data centers. Twenty years ago, data centers, such as the ones run by Facebook, Microsoft, Google, YouTube, and other internet service providers used 1 percent of all electricity generated. Now, the figure has increased to almost 2 percent. With increasing computerization, the development of autonomous vehicles, and the use of artificial intelligence, the share of electricity generation used by data centers is likely to increase even further.

Despite all these plans that will inevitably increase the

demand for electricity, few countries have plans in place for an expansion of power generation and distribution on a relevant scale.

As already mentioned, in an interview at the conference Codecon 2021, Elon Musk responded to a question from the audience regarding whether the power supply may become a bottleneck for the expansion of electromobility. Musk replied that electromobility will cause the demand for electricity to double and that investments will be needed in all parts of power grids.[13]

All countries that plan some form of large-scale conversion to electricity will have to significantly expand power generation and grid capacity, for e-mobility as well as for many other purposes.

With plans to turn countries sustainable in the coming decades, the lack of plans for the expansion of power production, distribution grids, and charging infrastructure represents a high risk. A continued shortage of electricity will threaten economic growth, affluence, and the conversion of transport systems and other systems to sustainable varieties.

It is about time that governments develop the necessary plans. Governments do not, by any means, need to finance the entire expansion. There are well-functioning energy markets. But this type of expansion will in many countries need large-scale and long-term support to create the stable market conditions that companies need

---

13 The question from the audience is asked a little more than fifty-nine minutes into the following video: https://www.youtube.com/watch?app=desktop&v=TcI6FaaDp8g.

to make investments. Exceptional expansion plans with a high degree of uncertainty are likely to need support from governments. In the case of large-scale expansion, investments often need to be made a decade or more before the generation resources come online.

Governments will need to take important roles, but it is at present not clear what the markets can achieve on their own and what roles governments will need to take to drive the development forward.

Forbidden Territory 3: Focus on Sustainability - Not Large-Scale Transformation

In 2018 Greta Thunberg became world famous overnight for going on a school strike and for arguing that political leaders had not done enough to combat climate change. Over the past decades, an increasing number of sustainability experts have put forward the same argument, but none of the experts or the politicians that have tried to turn the arguments of environmentalists into policy have provided a credible account of what needs to be done to transform the industrial systems of the present society to sustainable production and distribution systems. They have also failed to mention the magnitude of the investments and transformation efforts that will be necessary to succeed with the change.

Several professors and experts in various disciplines of sustainability argue that the technologies that must replace the unsustainable technologies of the present are already available and only need to be implemented. They say this as if all governments need to do to transform society would be to press a button to start a systematic transformation.

The technical and environmental focus and the arguments by sustainability and technology experts have created a vast territory of ignorance about the magnitude of investments and transformation activities and the nature of the coordinated and collective efforts that will become necessary to succeed.

The change will not primarily be a matter of technology development. The key aspect that will constitute the difference between success and failure will be the ability of governments to organize and finance the change. There are principles of development and transformation similar to laws of nature. Humans cannot get Niagara Falls to flow upwards, and we cannot drive development and societal change on a large scale without managed programs and large-scale financing.

The Apollo program was a large-scale program of technology and system development and use. But the factor that made the program successful was the ability of NASA to organize and manage it against a very ambitious timeline and the ability of the American government to put up the funding that made it possible to perform all the necessary development activities. Technology and system development resulted from the financing and organized approach, leading to the success of the Apollo program in only nine years.

The proponents of sustainability, Greta Thunberg, Sir David Attenborough, Al Gore, politicians belonging to green parties, and sustainability and technical experts at universities and at companies large and small have become subject to hyperthink.

They have been successful in their efforts to turn everyone's attention toward climate change and the increasing concentration of carbon dioxide in the atmosphere that is deemed to be the cause of global warming. If asked what needs to be done, none of the experts is likely to have a reply ready. At the same time, they have turned the world's attention away from the measures that need to be initiated to go through with the transformation.

From Insight to Action — Building Resources

To build a stable and sustainable society for the future change, leaders need to start to explore the areas of ignorance that have developed in the shadow of hyperthink. The market economy rests on a set of very sound principles. The market is the most efficient allocator of resources in many situations in society, but there is a need for government involvement in the financing of the large-scale transformation to sustainability.

Market-based development does not produce predictable results. For example, there have been organic products in stores for many decades, but they have not taken over the entire food market. Instead, they remain more expensive than mainstream food products, and they form a niche category. To make sure that most vehicles will be electric in 2050, large-scale change programs will be necessary. With a ban of the sales of new gasoline and diesel cars in 2035, most cars are likely to be electric by 2050.

In a way similar to how NASA managed the Apollo program from start to finish, a government agency needs to be given the responsibility for the management of the transformation in each country, and an international organization may have to take on the responsibility for international cooperation. Collaboration between countries would probably reduce the resources needed to go through with the change, and it is likely to speed up the process. This will not rule out competition.

Here, the UN or some other organization can play an important role in the organization of collaboration and coordination of development and implementation activities in such a way that all the necessary development steps will be taken. An organization should also ensure that production resources are built for the manufacturing of products that will be needed in large amounts throughout the transformation program. The UN already has some of the necessary experience, as it and its associated organizations have taken the lead in the development of equipment needed, for example, for large-scale operations to provide aid to victims of natural disasters. It, however, would need to rapidly develop all the skills and competencies needed to lead the change to sustainability, in the way NASA did when taking on the Apollo program.

It is easy to conclude that the UN does not have the necessary competence and that the organization may not be suitable to manage this responsibility, but there is no other organization that could take on this type of role. The alternative would be to establish a new organization with the task of coordinating development or coordinate efforts between countries without a transnational organization to do the job. It could perhaps be done via multilateral discussions and agreements between countries, but this is likely to take more time and be more costly.

Collaboration and competition are two necessary aspects in the development of markets, just like public and private funding complement each other. Both are necessary and serve different purposes. Public co-financing is needed at the early stages of development and when large-scale expansion is needed to handle a level of risk that cannot be handled by market-based players. Private funding can otherwise take care of most of the development in mature markets. Collaboration can be used to reduce the risk of duplication of effort. Competition can be used to make sure that companies develop cost-effective solutions.

Governments also need to take the responsibility for developing stable structures for systems for electric transportation, for the expansion of power generation and distribution, and for the mapping of the processes for the development of some of the most important technologies of the future. This will be important to reduce mass confusion and diminish the risk of creating speculation bubbles.

Change is always uncertain, but a number of changes will be necessary over the coming decades. The sooner governments and other leading organizations start to approach the challenges in a systematic and structured way, the higher the probability that the development and change efforts will be successful.

It will not be enough for people and experts to simply learn about the transformation process and discuss the facts related to this. The acquisition of knowledge and the development of a new way of speaking about an issue does not lead to change. For change to take place, transformation resources need to be built and large-scale change activities need to be started; this will require large-scale funding.

Orgware

The resources needed are sometimes referred to as "orgware," organizational resources consisting of individuals with the relevant background, knowledge, financing, and tools to start up and lead large-scale change activities.

In the case of sustainability, countries have built orgware for the research of environmental issues and small-scale mitigation on the national, regional, and municipal levels. There are government authorities that monitor pollution and set limits to the levels of emissions allowed. Authorities are responsible for the preservation of nature, and there are many non-governmental organizations that work with small-scale activities to promote the implementation of electromobility on a small scale or run projects to implement circular business models, also on a small scale. But there is no orgware ready to be used to take on the challenges of large-scale transformation.

NASA built orgware for the space programs, inside its own organization, but also by financing and managing external research and development activities and forcing contractors to build the competences and manpower of their own organizations to meet strict deadlines.

If Americans had been asked in 1961 if they were interested in participating in the Apollo program, most would most likely have said that they did not have the skills and that they did not know what the program was all about or how they could contribute. In 1969, four hundred thousand Americans were, or had been, part of the program. They had been given roles that they could fulfill, through the organizational process that was one important aspect of the development.

What is missing in the efforts to transform the world to sustainability are three very important things:

- Financing
- Change Management
- Organization — the creation of orgware, or organizational capital

But the most important aspect will be financing. Money not only makes the world go around. It fuels development and the progress of transformation activities, which in their turn drive the process of organization.

Business Development and Financing

More attention needs to be paid to the development of companies that will be able to grow and offer all the products and services needed. Many important innovations are developed by small companies without strong financial muscle. It often takes decades for small companies to grow and develop ecosystems and entire new industries. In the case of the space program, NASA has played an important role in the development of technologies and in the development of the space industry.

Companies with important technologies should be nurtured and strong ecosystems of partners should be built around them. The problem is that with the present goal of a very rapid transformation, there is little time to expand companies from start-ups to large companies, and there is definitely not any time to cover up for big mistakes or pitfalls in the development process.

In past innovation efforts, such as the Apollo program,

the forms of financing have varied depending on the challenges and the circumstances. Different models have been applied for different parts of the systems. In the early decades of the twentieth century, the American government financed the development and expansion of commercial air travel, and the payment for goods transportation was designed so as to incentivize airlines to also make room for a few passengers. Thus, the passenger airline industry was born through the creative application of incentives.

In the case of space technologies, NASA co-financed development projects, and competitive bidding was used to hand out contracts to the most competitive bidders. In the case of the development of computers, financing of development projects was used in combination with the purchases of the early generations of computers by the military, the IRS, and other US authorities.

The fact that many of the systems that were built through government financing have become privatized in later years does not mean that the market in the twenty-first century can finance the development of new technologies from the early stages or that the market can drive rapid and focused transformation processes.

Despite the fact that there are entrepreneurs who express an interest in building electric road networks, the large-scale roll-out may take longer, and the way forward could, if financing models are not carefully crafted, become fraught with bankruptcies and failures of companies that underestimate the risk and overestimate the willingness of customers to buy electric trucks and their ability to make profitable use of them. The belief in the power of the market has made even experienced and knowledgeable individuals believe that the market can work wonders, even in the early stages of development, but it cannot, and it will not. The market can only work wonders in combination with creative government financing.

One of the biggest challenges is the fact that electric vehicles at present are very expensive compared to petroleum-fueled ones, and it is possible that this situation will remain for many years into the future. Typically, an electric car costs 50 percent more than an equivalent gasoline car. The price of an electric van is almost twice the price of a diesel van, and electric heavy trucks cost three times as much as diesel alternatives. This is a type of situation where when other technologies were still in their infancy, government procurement contributed to building market volume and forced down prices.

The markets for electric vehicles are growing rapidly at present, but it will be difficult for households with smaller incomes to afford an electric car, and it will be even more difficult for companies in low-margin industries to pay for transportation by electric truck. The ability of different categories of customers to pay more for transportation has to be taken into account when decisions regarding the pace of the transformation are taken.

It is also true that a significant share of the market for

electric vehicles at present is held by hybrids that can also be driven on fossil fuels. This provides vehicles and their owners with the best of two worlds — electric propulsion most of the time and infinite range without frequent charging stops when needed. The plan is to ban hybrids and go for 100 percent electric. It may be difficult for some groups of customers to change to fully electric vehicles, especially people without charging opportunities where they park.

Risk of Failure

Politicians may think that drivers need to adapt to the need to abolish fossil-fuel vehicles, but convenient transportation solutions contribute to productivity. Reforms need to be made in a way that resonates with the needs of citizens, because if people cannot remain productive, the prosperity of our present society will erode — quite rapidly.

A rapid growth of fleets of electric vehicles reduces the time available to expand infrastructure; it may be impossible to expand rapidly enough to facilitate the charging of all vehicles. If expansion hits a solid wall in the form of a shortfall of electricity, people are likely to lose interest in electromobility and push for a return to petroleum-fueled cars and trucks, even though this is not sustainable.

The problem here is once more the pressing timetable for the change. Many things need to be done in parallel. There will not be much time available to experiment with different financing alternatives, business models, or various technical solutions or system configurations. In the Apollo program, NASA developed the financing models and technical solutions very rapidly and made them work throughout. A similar approach will be needed with respect to the present change.

Government Financing Strengthens Markets

As we can see from the examples already given and those that will be provided later in the text, government financing does not detract power from the market. On the contrary, it strengthens the market and contributes to its ability to work its magic. Hyperthink has been at work putting forward incomplete arguments, such as the idea by sustainability experts and activists that more needs to be done, without ever specifying the exact activities that need to be performed.

More definitely needs to be done, but more needs to be done in very specific areas, and activities need to be organized and financed in ways that optimize the outcome.

Very slowly, governments, experts, journalists, and citizens at large are beginning to realize that countries have done far too little to prepare for the conversion.

As Bill Gates argues that the transformation to a sustainable society will require countries to double or triple power production and Elon Musk admits that electromobility alone will require countries to double generation capacity, decision-makers will have to take in these predictions and ask themselves how the challenge can be tackled.

5

Examples of Hyperthink

Hyperthink is not new. Examples can be found throughout history. Toward the end of the twentieth century and in the twenty-first century, it has taken on previously unseen dimensions and hindered the development of new technologies and systems. Political correctness has become an accepted tool to abolish debate and diversity of views. System development is often based on the application of single ideas, rather than on a system perspective.

Many believe that technology development is making faster progress than ever before. This has been true for the technologies that started their development fifty or one hundred years ago and that have matured in the past decades. In the case of the technologies that are needed to drive economic growth and develop the society of the future, it is not true.

Resources need to be focused, not spread thinly across a rapidly increasing number of areas.

The March of Folly — Examples from History

There are numerous examples throughout history of situations where leaders have made gigantic mistakes and been led astray by megalomania and a lack of a sense of responsibility.

The complexity of developing a sustainable society and the ambition of politicians, experts, and some business leaders to downplay the complexity and portray the transformation as something that can be achieved over the next few decades, without any cost or sacrifice for the present generations, has put countries in a very difficult situation. Great investment must be made in large-scale change programs, a fact that is going to become increasingly obvious to everyone in the coming years.

It has become obvious in large parts of Europe that the energy policies of several countries in the past decade have led to shortages of electricity that in the past two winters have sent prices soaring. At the same time, in 2022, the environmental ministers of the EU have decided to ban the sales of new gasoline and diesel cars from 2035, a decision that will dramatically increase the demand for electricity and send prices even higher.

A similar situation exists in California, where air regulators have decided to ban the sales of gasoline cars from 2035, a decision made in the fall of 2022 that was followed a few weeks later by the plea from utilities to owners of electric cars not to charge over the Labor Day weekend.

These examples indicate that governments need to get their act together and develop policies based on reality, taking into account the actual capacity of power generation and other systems, and plan change programs based on an understanding of what can realistically be achieved given the available resources.

In the book *The March of Folly,* historian Barbara Tuchman describes how leaders throughout history have pursued policies that have gone contrary to self-interest. We would, perhaps, have thought that this type of example belongs in the past and that mistakes were made possible due to the autocratic leadership in those days. We see, however, that groupthink and hyperthink are strong in the present society as well. Despite the availability of all kinds of information, the use of social media and the internet does not seem to broaden the perspectives of most people, but rather the opposite.

In the cases analyzed by Tuchman, the flawed strategies and decisions led to the loss of influence, humiliation, and enormous economic losses over the long term. The most recent examples recounted in *The March of Folly* are the decisions that led to the Vietnam War.

The prototypical event described by Tuchman is the decision by the leaders of Troy to take the Trojan Horse through the city gates and the subsequent conquest of the city by the Greek soldiers who hid inside it. Tuchman describes the act of taking the horse as a trophy and bringing it into the city as an act of folly that led to the fall of Troy. It is possible to draw parallels with the decisions to adopt sustainable technologies. These decisions have been made without considering the system-wide effects of applying new technologies on a large scale and without considering the amount of electricity and other expansion and conversion activities that will be needed to fuel growing fleets of electric vehicles.

After describing the trojan horse debacle, Tuchman goes on to describe three prolonged periods of political folly that had disastrous consequences for those who pursued these policies:

- The frivolous lifestyles of the popes, which led to the Reformation and the Protestant secession (1470–1530).
- The American Revolution and the loss of the American colonies by the British (1763–1783).
- The Vietnam War, a war that the United States could not win. The decisions that led to the war started, according to Tuchman, immediately after the Second World War (1945–1973).

These examples of the persistent errors of politicians and religious leaders could be seen as a foreshadowing of what is to come. Is it possible that the period of growth the world has experienced for almost eighty years after the Second World War has been made possible by a set of very specific circumstances, that can best be described as *lucky*, ones that are now in the process of being replaced by a more complex technical and political landscape that increases the probability of large and possibly fatal mistakes?

Will future generations add the present period to the examples described by Tuchman and list the attempt to change twenty-first-century society to sustainability as another failure, one that may perhaps even surpass those described by Tuchman as examples of folly and failed policies?

Examples from Twenty-First-Century Politics

After the Second World War, development was driven according to an uncomplicated formula. Governments did whatever was necessary to prepare their countries for the demands of the future, and there was a limited set of alternatives, which made the decisions relatively straightforward compared to the present. The existence of a limited set of alternatives was important and is probably the biggest difference compared to the present situation.

While technical and economic development has brought forward many new technologies and opportunities for the future, the use of fossil fuels and the pursuit of resource-demanding economic growth have created pollution, climate change, and the threat of resource depletion. As the number of alternative routes of development has grown, it has become increasingly difficult for decision-makers and experts to build a coherent picture of the present challenges and the way forward.

Governments need to implement policies to reduce the emissions of carbon dioxide and other greenhouse gases and reduce the use of resources. At the same time, they need to continue to drive economic growth because this creates affluence and the financial means to pursue the transformation to sustainability.

The idea that it should be possible to put economic growth to a stop and still transform society to sustainability is an example of hyperthink. The very large investments that will be necessary to create a sustainable society can only be financed as long as countries experience economic growth.

On the surface this may seem to be a relatively straight-forward task. Continue the strategies of the past while implementing green technologies, increase the use of ICT to drive growth, and watch a beautiful future unfold before our eyes. What could be simpler?

The problem, however, seems to be that the development of the future will have to rely on a new logic and organization of development. Over the past decade, it has become increasingly obvious that leaders and experts have failed to develop a sound formula for the development. This failure to formulate effective policies can be observed in the form of a number of examples of failures. When looked at closely, it is obvious that hyperthink is at work. The development challenges have been described in overly simplified terms, with dangerous consequences.

The Implementation of Wind Power and the Switch to Russian Gas

Wind power seems like a superb idea. The development has been moving forward since the 1970s. The country that for a long time led the development is Denmark, the small country that at the beginning of the twenty-first century produced more than 50 percent of the world's wind power.

The development of wind turbines in Denmark has been going on since 1891, when the first wind generator was built in a project funded by the Danish government. After the oil embargo of the 1970s, the government decided to jump-start the development of wind power and reduce its dependence on coal. It implemented a number of financing and collaboration programs to support wind. This led to an expansion that in the early twenty-first century resulted in a 50 percent share of power generation from wind. Denmark seemed to have found the formula for making power generation sustainable.

Wind turbines have the advantage of not emitting any carbon dioxide in the operation phase. The disadvantage is that the technology, like solar-generated electricity, is intermittent. Power is only generated when there is suffi-cient wind.

Power consumption goes on at all times. Production

plants and cities, with their offices and shopping centers, need power also on days when there is little or no wind. For this reason, there is a need for backup power. Previous power sources, such as fossil fuels, nuclear power plants, and hydroelectric plants, can function on a 24/7 basis.

Power grids also need to be balanced at a certain frequency. The heavy turbines of nuclear, coal, and hydro-electric plants contribute to balancing the grid, while the frequency may fluctuate with the fluctuations in the supply of wind electricity. This creates the risk that the power supply breaks down when there is insufficient wind.

The idea is that with many wind turbines spread out across large land areas, there will always be enough wind in some parts of the system, which will keep frequencies in balance and produce enough electricity to satisfy demand. One problem seems to be that this is not always the case. In Europe it happens that there are similar weather conditions north of the Alps, creating a risk of wind lull in large parts of Europe, as was the case for several weeks in the autumn of 2022.

With a population of some five million people, the power produced in Denmark only amounts to 30 TWh per year. A limited amount of backup power is needed, and the balancing power can, to some extent, be supplied from abroad. In the early years of Denmark's expansion of wind power, some of this balancing power was supplied by the Swedish nuclear reactors located right opposite the Danish coast.

Germany started its transformation to sustainable energy sources later than the Danes. In 1995, the amount of onshore wind power produced in Germany was 1.5 TWh. This figure had increased to 100 TWh by 2019, and the German government had decided to close the country's last nuclear plants by 2021. Similar policies of expanding wind power have been pursued in other northern European countries as well, for example in Sweden, where wind generation had increased to 27 TWh in 2020, 16 percent of a total annual production of 150 TWh. In the years leading up to 2020 a number of nuclear reactors and fossil-fuel powerplants have been closed in the ambition to create a sustainable and risk-free power supply.

Only a small number of experts on electricity systems seem to have realized that there is a tremendous risk for Europe in relying heavily on wind power. Through the autumn of 2022, imports of Russian gas had declined due to the Russian war on Ukraine, and there were protracted periods of low wind, which resulted in very high electricity prices, not only in Germany but also in neighboring countries with grids that were connected to the German grids.

German power production and consumption are the highest in Europe; only that of France can rival the size of the German generation. With low winds and high prices of power through the autumn and with twenty-six of the fifty-six nuclear reactors in France inactive due to maintenance or repairs, the German government had to postpone the decommissioning of the three remaining German reactors until April 2023.

Wind generation is a cost-effective alternative, but the large-scale use requires backup resources in the form of plannable generation resources or large facilities for battery storage that can be used during periods of low wind. This need for backup resources needs to be added to the cost of wind power, and it would dramatically change the cost profile if large facilities for battery storage would be built for this purpose.

The standstill of many nuclear reactors contributed to the difficulties. This indicates a need for redundance also in the resources for plannable power generation. Power sources with different production profiles need to balance, and the development needs to be based on thorough risk analyses that take different scenarios into account.

Lithium-ion batteries are still at an early phase in their development, and production volumes are relatively small. Batteries are still expensive, and the cost of building large-scale resources for storage would be too high.

It is possible to utilize used electric car batteries for storage, but the number of used batteries available is low and the need for storage would be very large, considering the large amount of generation capacity from wind and solar that has already been installed and the expansion plans for the future. The number of electric cars that are more than ten years old and in need of new batteries is small; it will take many years for the number of batteries to grow so that the need could be covered.

It is not clear the amount of battery storage that will be needed. For the moment, storage resources for *peak shaving* are becoming viable. This means storage for a few seconds between very short peaks and troughs in production. Very large resources would be needed to cover the fluctuations over twenty-four hours, and even larger ones would be needed to store electricity to cover variations across a week. To make it possible to store enough electricity to weather a few weeks of wind lull, the need for battery capacity would be extreme.

The only fossil-free generation technology that can be used to balance grids on a large scale is nuclear. Hydroelectric power can do this as well, but the remaining resources are limited. Compared to the use of batteries to cover up periods of low wind, nuclear production is cost-effective. It is difficult to get around the thought that nuclear may be the only alternative that can complement the expansion of wind power over the coming decades.

It may be argued that it was a lucky circumstance for Europe that the Russian invasion of Ukraine happened in 2022 and not after April 2023, when Germany had already closed its last three nuclear reactors. This may lead to a dire energy situation in Europe in the years to come, especially if gas supply problems return.

It would be disastrous for Europe if France were to follow in the footsteps of Germany and start to dismantle its nuclear plants and heavily expand wind power. It is somewhat ironic that Germany seems to trade its dependence on the supply of gas from Russia for a dependence on France to secure the balancing of European power grids during periods of wind lull. Let us hope that France will not have to put a large number of its reactors to a standstill in the years to come, in the way that happened in the autumn of 2022.

The decision by the previous German government to build close bonds with Russia to secure the gas supply seems to have been tantamount to bringing the Trojan horse into Troy. Building a reliance on wind power without securing significant backup resources may be another hard-earned experience for Europe. Since governments have no opportunity to control either wind or Russian foreign policy, the safest bet seems to have been for Germany to keep running its remaining nuclear reactors for a few more years instead of decommissioning them, as they have now done.

With the large-scale expansion of intermittent technologies for power generation, the expansion and balancing of power grids have become *team sports*. Earlier, countries could, to a large extent, make decisions independent of one another, knowing that generation could be controlled. At present, countries with a large share of wind and solar generation run the risk of having to rely on other countries for the power supply and balancing of grids when generation from intermittent sources is low. It stands to reason that all countries cannot rely primarily on wind and solar technologies. The question is to what extent these technologies can be expanded without causing too large a risk to power systems.

It also seems to be the case that wind and solar power cannot be relied upon to balance grids when many heavy industrial plants are on the receiving end of power cables. Intermittent technologies are better suited to provide power for city lighting and the lighting of shopping malls, where it is not a problem if there are small fluctuations in the supply. When it comes to supplying heavy industry and sensitive hospital equipment with electricity, the quality and stability of the power supply are important.

The limited risk of incidents in nuclear plants must be weighed against the high risk of high prices of power and unbalanced grids that may even break down, with disastrous consequences for European affluence.

The shortage of electricity and the high prices experienced in Europe are otherwise likely to cost the countries of the EU dearly over the coming years. The plans to transform transport systems to electric vehicles are also at stake. High prices will make it more difficult for companies and households to finance purchases of electric vehicles, make it more expensive to operate fleets of electric cars, buses, and trucks, and reduce the amount of money and capital available for other purposes. This may cause a recession or depression, during which it will be difficult to run a swift transformation to a new and more expensive set of technologies.

The logical alternative at this point, considering the very difficult situation the world has ended up in, would be to start up as many of the decommissioned German reactors as will be needed to maintain a stable power supply, and develop a new plan for the German *Energiewende* in collaboration with neighboring countries. As Europe's electricity grids are connected, the decisions of one large country will inevitably have repercussions for its neighbors.

It is possible that the success of Denmark in implementing wind power on a relatively small scale may be difficult to transplant on a large scale across Europe or the United States. A large-scale dependence on wind may destabilize the entire power grid of a continent.[14]

Electromobility

The subject of electromobility has been touched upon in several places in the book. So far, the share of electric

---

14 I thank Professor Jan Blomgren for enhancing my understanding of the need to balance electricity grids. In his Swedish book Allt du behöver veta om Sveriges elförsörjning (All You Need to Know About Sweden's Power Supply), he explains the intricacies of balancing power grids. The Swedish government has for decades pursued an energy policy similar to that of Germany, consisting of closing down nuclear reactors without securing enough generation and transmission resources in the remaining power system. This has led to a situation where the country has access to relatively large power resources in the north, while the amount of power in the south is not sufficient. In 2022, prices increased dramatically in the south, largely due to the need to import electricity from Germany and the high prices spread to the north, that did not expect this type of development. Now Sweden, like Germany, is facing an uncertain energy future while at the same time the governments in both these countries have high ambitions for the transformation to electromobility.

and hybrid cars is small, and no country has experienced either the load on electricity grids or the demand for chargers that will arise when the majority of cars and a growing share of trucks and buses will be charged on a daily basis.

Norway is the country that leads the transformation globally. The change to electromobility started there in 1994, as the Norwegian electric car Think was launched at the opening of the Olympic Winter Games in Lillehammer. Norway also has the highest per capita generation of electricity in Europe with 125 TWh of electricity generated for a population of five million. This is 21 percent of the German generation of 600 TWh, for a population of eighty-three million and 38 percent of the UK production for a population of sixty-seven million. Norwegian power generation per person is almost three times that of Germany and five times the per capita power production of the UK. Thus, Norwegian power is both abundant and inexpensive and the government has strong reasons to promote electromobility and subsidize it generously. The more cars and trucks that are driven on electricity, the more of its oil can be exported to earn income to finance the subsidies of electric car purchases. Few other countries are likely to enjoy a situation where subsidies of electric vehicles can be paid for by an increase in exports of some other source of increased income. At present, the share of electric cars in Norway amounts to almost 15 percent.

In Europe overall, the share of electric cars is in the

area of 3 to 4 percent. This is the share in Germany, France, and the UK. As has been mentioned earlier in the text, the regular charging of all forty-eight million German cars would require more than 100 TWh of electricity, and if all trucks and buses would be driven on electricity, some 50 percent more would be needed.

The German winters are also cold. When I lived in southern Germany in 2003, the region experienced a cold spell lasting several weeks that made the cooling liquid in my car freeze due to insufficient amounts of glycol. Temperatures hovered in the area of -10 degrees C. With vehicle fleets consisting of a large share of electric vehicles with present-day technology, countries would experience an increase in power consumption of a large share of the vehicles during such cold temperatures. A share of all vehicles would experience a reduced range of up to 20 percent, which would increase the need for electricity to charge those vehicles over the short winter period.

Power generation is, however, not the only bottleneck that will arise as countries convert transport systems to electromobility. Elon Musk, in the previously mentioned interview at Codecon 2021, argued that countries will have to double resources for power generation. He mentioned also that the expansion of all parts of electricity grids will be needed.[15]

15https://www.google.com/search?q=elon+musk+codecon+2021+you-tube&rlz=1C1BYYL_svSE956SE956&oq=elon&aqs=chrome.0.69i59j69i57j35i-39j46i131i433i512j0i131i433i512j0i131i433j46i175i199i512j69i61.1056j0j7&-sourceid=chrome&ie=UTF-8.

It should be noted here that no auto company has any influence over the planning or execution of all these activities, and the decision-makers who should make it happen are not aware of the need to act or what decisions need to be made. In any country, thousands of municipalities, utilities, real estate companies, operators of charging infrastructure, and other stakeholders will have to engage in expansion activities. This is a very risky situation for a company like Tesla, which is entirely dependent on the continued growth of the sales of electric cars and trucks.

There are also incumbents in the car industry that are investing heavily in building a position in the electric car market. Volvo Cars has decided to stop producing cars with gasoline and diesel engines from 2030, converting to electric cars 100 percent. This is a very risky move as the company only launched its first fully electric car in 2021, and we do not know at present if the ongoing increase in electric car sales can continue to a complete conversion in the time span decided by the EU and Californian authorities.

These types of measures will also be extremely risky as the automotive industry is very important for many countries. There are parts of Europe where 20 percent of households depend on auto companies or their suppliers for their income.

To convert the present transport systems to electro-mobility, the following development activities need to be performed and changes need to be made:

- All cars will need to be charged whenever they need charging, regardless of where they are. Chargers, fast and slow, or electric road systems will be needed for all cars.

- Enough generation capacity will be needed to cover charging needs at all times. Generation capacity in most countries will have to increase by 50 percent or more. Power will be needed to charge vehicles, but also for the power-intensive production of lithium-ion batteries. A doubling of the generation capacity in the United States would mean the installation of enough capacity to produce 4,000 TWh of electricity per year.

- Power grids will need to be expanded to facilitate the charging needed.

- Power grids need to become digitized to make it possible to optimize the utilization of electricity and use electric vehicle batteries as a backup to provide extra capacity and balance grids through vehicle-to-grid (V2G) solutions. Digitization of grids will make it possible to communicate between control systems in order to turn on or turn off charging and other activities, depending on the demand for power at any given time. V2G will allow cars to be connected to the power grid so the electricity in their batteries can be used to sell back power and balance grids at times of high demand. While it may not be a good idea to rely on this type of solution on a large scale, it can be applied on a limited scale.

- Hundreds of thousands of administrators and decision-makers in public organizations and private companies need to receive training to be able to take on roles in development and transformation projects for electromobility.
- Businesses need to be developed that will supply all the products and services needed. Tens of thousands of existing companies need to be converted to other lines of business or closed as the demand for their products goes down through the change to electric vehicles.
- Development and transformation programs will have to be started locally, regionally, and nationally to make sure that all necessary tasks and activities will be taken care of.

The above may not sound like an extreme challenge, but it will be a much larger development program than the Apollo program. The latter involved the production of a small number of Saturn V rockets, capsules for the crew, moon landers, and the other equipment necessary for each mission. Other necessary components of the program were a launch ramp, a building where a few rockets could be built at a time, a control center, space suits, and some other equipment. The key was that everything was needed only in small quantities and the cost of each item was not important.

The change to electric vehicles involves much larger numbers and development challenges that are very difficult to predict and manage. For the conversion to electromobility in the United States, some 280 million cars and several million transport vehicles need to be changed to electric varieties, a corresponding number of chargers need to be installed, and the electricity grids in each local area need to be expanded, in particular for the charging of heavy vehicles and for fast charging of cars, but perhaps also to facilitate the charging of large numbers of cars at low or medium speed. Extensive systems of electric roads are also likely to be needed.

Very large volumes of products and components will be needed, and the price of each is very important indeed, as households and companies will have to be able to afford to buy vehicles and use the electrified transport systems. They also need to have sufficient amounts of money left to cover other needs once transportation has been paid for.

Brexit

Technology development and innovation need favorable business environments, good conditions for trade, and other circumstances that benefit investment, economic growth, and prosperity in general. For this reason, it is relevant to discuss Brexit in this context, a process that has reduced the financial strength of the UK and Europe. We may think whatever we like about economic growth and big finance, but within the present economic system, on which most of us are dependent for our daily bread, both are necessary to maintain the affluence and prosperity we enjoy now and expect in the future. More ingenious schemes than Brexit will be needed to develop a sustainable economy that can both contribute to building the future and improve the quality of people's lives in the long run.

The EU and the organization's predecessors were formed to unify Europe after two world wars. The process started with the forming of the Coal and Steel Union in 1952. The European Union was formed in 1993.

The advantage of a union is not only that it will contribute to peaceful development. A larger market reduces barriers to trade, and it benefits all members. One of the advantages is that people can move freely and work in different countries, which increases the availability of personnel. In the more affluent countries, it increases access to low-wage labor and more citizens can rise to more qualified positions and thereby create more value.

Another advantage is that countries can trade goods and services freely across borders, without incurring the extra cost of tariffs that make products and services more expensive. The result is that people and companies can buy things from the most efficient suppliers and choose between a larger number of attractive alternatives. The red tape connected to trade will be reduced, which reduces the cost of each transaction and improves the efficiency of the economy.

The downside of the situation is that the advantages

are not apparent to all citizens. People need some understanding of economics to see that open markets and the free movement of goods and services benefit everyone. On the surface, it may seem as if there are mostly disadvantages for affluent countries and that people in countries with low wages and weaker economies get all the benefits. This is because people from low-wage economies can move to more prosperous countries and compete for many of the low-paying jobs.

It may then seem as if they are taking jobs away from citizens, when in fact they, to a large extent, may work in jobs that most of the people of the host country do not want. Guest workers offer valuable labor in areas where there would otherwise be a shortage.

This was the case in the UK in the years leading up to the Brexit referendum. People noticed that a lot of employees in service occupations, such as builders, drivers, shop assistants, and restaurant and café workers, came from other EU countries, in particular from Poland, and worried that this increased the competition for jobs. Many concluded that the large influx of foreign workers was a cause behind unemployment among the British and that the foreigners represented a threat.

Some political parties picked up these sentiments, turned them into policy, and started to campaign to take Britain out of the EU. The advantages of opening up markets are likely to appear early in the process. Significant economic growth is created gradually as barriers to trade are removed and people take advantage of the opportunities. The increase in the returns from an open market is likely to become smaller over time as most actors in the economy have taken advantage of the opportunities offered, but the disadvantages of trade barriers and barriers to the free flow of labor all come back at once when borders are closed. This is what happened to the UK as the country left the EU in 2020.

One of the consequences was that the volume of imported goods declined by 30 percent twelve months after Brexit. While this may be seen to benefit the British economy, the exports fell even more, by almost 50 percent, which meant that many companies lost a large share of their revenue, and many went out of business.

In addition to this, financial services companies took a blow. More than 10 percent of British financial assets were moved to other countries and many banks and financial institutions left Britain. Before Brexit, London was known as the financial capital of the world, a position it has now lost and that it will most likely be impossible to regain.

Since Brexit, the UK economy has not only suffered from reduced trade and the reductions of its financial sector, but also from a shortage of labor, especially in low-paying jobs, that was caused by sending foreign workers back to their home countries. The transport sector has suffered heavily from a shortage of drivers, and it is difficult to fill all vacant positions with British applicants. This results in higher transport prices, a reduction in service levels, and reduced productivity in the economy at large.

Much more can be said about the reasons behind Brexit and its consequences, but this is not a book about Brexit as such. Brexit is an example of hyperthink. Boris Johnson and other leading politicians who drove the process found a grievance among a large share of the British people and saw an opportunity to seize power by promoting Brexit and pushing the process forward to a referendum. They did this despite its vast negative consequences for the country and for many of the people who voted in favor of Brexit.

The promotion of Brexit, like the other examples of policies in this book, is based on mass confusion, the inability of large numbers of people to make sense of a complex reality. Instead of seeing through the false promises, many chose to vote for a simplistic and populistic solution. The changes that were achieved through Brexit resulted in the opposite type of development compared to what voters were promised. Instead of strengthening the British economy and making large numbers of jobs available to British workers, Brexit has led to reduced economic growth, a loss of job opportunities, and increased unemployment.

Great Britain — Greater EU?

Success in the modern world is all about organization and financing. Britain did not become great only because of the greatness of the people on the island on the European side of the Atlantic. To a massive extent, the empire contributed to the greatness of Britain, and so did the fact that the country was well organized. The institutions of British society, such as democracy and a well-functioning legal system, extended out to the colonies, made it an empire of great financial and political power.

Even if the EU is not perfect, it is a strong and relatively well-organized economic and political power, and it can draw on the resources of all its member states to achieve important goals. Sometimes this leads to controversy between states, but this could also be a strength. Diversity adds competence and a variety of resources.

The economic advantages of the union become even clearer when it is considered that a large share of the organizational and trade links with other European countries are provided through the membership. These come with the advantage of a minimum of regulations of trade, and labor mobility. When a country exits the union, it also has to organize new links with other countries, which is a lengthy and resource-consuming process of negotiating agreements and building administrative procedures and routines both in the exiting country and in countries it wants to do business with.

It is unlikely that the UK will become more successful on its own than it could become as a member of the EU. Going back to a situation that resembles the past may not be such a good idea when important aspects that contributed to the greatness of the days gone by are missing in the modern setup. For the people of the UK, Brexit has been a hard-earned experience that has had a strongly negative impact on the economy and the job market.

6

Hyperthink a Force of Nature - The Entropy of Thought

Hyperthink is not a new phenomenon. It seems as if the widespread use of the internet and social media has contributed to a reduced amount of constructive debate, and it has increased mass confusion as an increasing number of people take ideas primarily from like-minded individuals.

The complexity that has boomed over the past decades, boosted by the use of digital tools, has contributed to the development. It is becoming harder to make sense of reality, and there are too many topics for people to keep abreast of.

This boils down to an increasing probability of suboptimal decision-making, and it creates the risk that development will go in the opposite direction, in several senses, compared to the one people have become used to.

Making Sense of a More Complex World

From the analysis by psychologists related earlier, it seems almost inevitable that people will believe in false, or highly questionable, information. With increasing complexity and a growing number of issues to keep abreast of, it becomes more difficult to think through all aspects of the development of the future, study relevant technologies, read books and articles, check facts, and make sound judgments. It is also impossible for individuals to influence development in each area in the way that they may want to. The most likely strategy for most people will be to follow the development in some areas of particular interest to them, vote in elections, and hope for the best.

The post-war period, up until the turn of the present century, was unique in a very important sense. Many technologies whose development had started fifty or one hundred years earlier, and in some cases more, were maturing to become cost-effective general-purpose technologies. The development had not gone on long enough for the technologies and systems to proliferate immensely and create a large number of varieties available today that make it difficult to develop political and financial strategies. The number of issues that had to be dealt with by politicians, business leaders, administrators, and decision-makers had not become so complex that it was too difficult to make constructive decisions.

One example of a development that was started

relatively late is the development of the first mobile phone systems. The reason why these systems could be developed so rapidly was that the communication technologies needed had already been developed across many decades for emergency services, based on radio technology. This development had been going on since the early years of the twentieth century.

The launch was not an immediate success. When the first generations of mobile phones were launched, the phones were large, including batteries weighing several kilos, and the price of phones and subscriptions was high. The cost of making even a brief call amounted to several dollars. Few subscribers signed up in the first few years. The operators faced the alternatives of promoting the systems more strongly or closing the services. Due to the amount of money that had already been pumped into the systems for substations and other facilities, the Nordic operators decided to make another risky bet. They started to subsidize phones when people signed subscriptions, hoping that the investment would pay back later as subscribers used their phones and paid their substantial bills.

Initially, it was primarily companies that subscribed, those that could derive business advantages from having access to mobile phones. I worked as a travel guide on coach tours to tourist destinations in Europe. The bus companies I worked with used mobile phones in coaches back in Sweden to redirect drivers to pick up new groups of customers when someone called who needed a coach at short notice. That way they could increase earnings and boost profit. Drivers no longer had to go to the office to get instructions. Valuable time was saved, and companies that bought mobile phones got a competitive advantage.

The travel agencies I worked with used mobile phones to maintain an emergency service that travelers could call when their coaches were late to pick them up. The employee responsible for the emergency service would sometimes be called up in the middle of the night by a customer worried about the coach being late. Instead of having a person in the office at 2 a.m. when connecting buses were going through Sweden to pick travelers up for departures from Malmö, the person responsible for the emergency service could solve the customer's problem and go back to sleep.

These are examples of early advantages of mobile phones that made customers sign up despite the high price and the size and weight of the phones.

Development Financing 2023

At present, there are tens of thousands of alternative technical solutions that can be developed, and financing bodies, for example in the EU, contribute to technology development by financing tens of thousands of development projects for a few years at the early stages.

Projects that are financed through development

programs, co-financed by the EU, such as in the Horizon Europe program, are typically not followed up by continued financing after the projects are finished, and results may not be further developed or used once they have been created. In the present Horizon Europe program, the contributions from the EU amount to 95.5 billion euros for the period of 2022 to 2027. Another disadvantage is that the limits that are set on the financing of each project are not likely to take development all the way to fully developed products, systems, or services.

Unlike the Apollo program, in which the goal was to develop all the technologies and solutions needed to the stage where they could be used in space missions, project associations that apply for EU funding may face a funding limit of 10 million euros.

The Apollo program was a more focused effort with a clearly defined goal. To reach the goal, development projects had to get enough funding to create technologies that could be used, and results had to be taken forward in several steps after the development of an initial prototype or product. Through the program, the resulting technologies were developed several steps further than is likely to be the case in EU-funded projects.

Successful Development Programs of the Past

In 1961, President John F. Kennedy challenged the United States to send a man to the moon and bring him safely back to Earth before the end of the decade. Most of the necessary technologies did not exist in 1961, so they had to be developed through the program. NASA built the competence to take responsibility for meeting the challenge and for managing technology development through the formulation of development assignments, procurement of components and products, and co-financing of these investments to the degree necessary for the program to succeed.

In the Apollo program, projects were closely monitored, and the results were rapidly taken care of and integrated into the different parts of the systems that had to be built for the different missions.

In the case of the development of computers, many steps were taken, consisting of building a computer with a specific purpose. The technologies necessary to achieve the goal had to be developed as part of the project. The Army Ballistics Research Laboratory commissioned the development of the first computer, against the advice of the United States computing establishment, to calculate firing tables for the artillery. According to Ruttan, they gambled on a technology that had not been tested, and the Mauchly-Eckert machine, the Electronic Numerical Integrator and Calculator (ENIAC), became ready in 1946.[16] Several subsequent projects took computer development step-by-step further toward turning computers into cost-effective machines that do more than simply calculate.

---

16   Vernon W. Ruttan. *Is War Necessary for Economic Growth?* Oxford University Press 2006.

These projects forced IBM and other computer companies to solve technical challenges in ways that resulted in development leaps, and they gradually contributed to building the computer industry of the United States into world leadership.

The development of the ARPANET is another example of a program with the goal of developing the technologies necessary for the communication of information between research centers across the United States. The program included, for example, developing the technologies for breaking messages up into bits of information and for sending the different bits through a network of routers to receiving computers, where the bits were once more assembled into the original message.

To make communication possible, IP addresses had to be developed and so did the technologies for sending messages through networks of routers using this addressing technology.

Ineffective Systems for Innovation

Despite the urgent need to develop electromobility, create the necessary technologies, implement new transport systems, and expand power generation, charging infrastructure, and grid capacity, no specific goals have been defined for the development.

Project partners may apply for financing of projects based on their own interests, but the officials responsible for the programs do not make sure that projects fit together to create a coherent result. Some progress is achieved, but there is no vision of an overall goal comparable to that of sending a man to the moon.

Instead, financing is provided to applicants who present their projects in a persuasive way and who have been able to build associations consisting of the most experienced partners. It is by no means certain that the projects that receive funding are the ones that will be needed to take the next step of development, or that the different efforts financed together will lead to the necessary leaps of innovation.

The EU has been built on the premise that governments were not allowed to distort competition, and for this reason development can only be supported at the early stages of the processes. All competitors must be given the same chance of getting their projects financed.

According to this logic, it would distort the dynamics of the market if the EU or national governments would follow through and finance the development of fully fledged systems. There is a lack of insight into the fact that technologies and systems have not been developed in this way in the past or that the approach is not likely to succeed. It gives the impression that rapid progress is being made, but this is an illusion. Many activities are started and driven forward up to a point, but very little in terms of fully developed technologies or technical breakthroughs come out at the other end.

When the EU decided to ban the sales of new gasoline and diesel cars from 2035, it had not occurred to leaders or administrators that they may have to investigate whether this is possible. It is taken for granted that ambitious results — in fact, any conceivable result, as it seems — can be achieved without planning, goal-oriented management, or substantial public financing.

It is as if the results dreamed up through hyperthink could be turned into reality through a disorganized process with insufficient funding.

Complexity — a Law of Nature

In his book *The Collapse of Complex Societies*, archaeologist Joseph Tainter presented the idea of the increasing complexity of societies as the reason behind the collapse of historical civilizations, like the Roman Empire, and the Mayan and Incan cultures. This has, since the book's publication in 1988, become the accepted theory, replacing previous theories, such as the one that the Roman Empire was toppled by the influx of peoples from Asia, and that other historic societies collapsed, for example, because of extended periods of drought.

These events were decisive, but the same type of event had successfully been dealt with by these civilizations earlier in their development. It was at a later stage, when the societies had become more complex, that these events led to collapse. The cost of dealing with challenges increases as organizations and societies become increasingly complex; more people need to be involved in decision-making, and few individuals can have an overview of the entire system, draw the relevant conclusions, and rapidly make decisions about countermeasures.

According to Tainter, complexity increases as a by-product of development. We see it in our society and in the proliferation of all kinds of technologies that contribute to a rapid growth of complexity, and it reduces our ability to handle it. With increasing complexity, the cost of mitigating threats and handling issues increases as a larger number of specialized individuals are required to take part. It slows down decision-making and increases the cost of administration due to an increasing number of authorities and experts who must oversee and regulate different areas.

Hyperthink—An Inevitable Consequence of Complexity?

In an increasingly complex society, it becomes more difficult to make sense of the world. The ability to reach a large share of the information and knowledge that has been produced throughout history is bound to convince people that the present is only the beginning of a development that will continue for generations.

But information and knowledge do not create the future. The future is created through technical breakthroughs and economic growth, and to achieve this there is a need to focus resources on the most important technologies.

To the average person, it is likely taken for granted that the technology development that we have experienced over the past decades can continue in the absence of large-scale government financing of innovation. A significant share of the large-scale development programs that brought about the technologies we have access to at present was completed before most citizens alive today were born. The Apollo program, the development of computers, and the ARPANET are only a few examples of the large-scale development programs that built the foundation of today's technology landscape. Similar programs will be needed to develop the technologies of the future.

In the present day, when opinions and beliefs are amplified through social media, people will get the impression that the development is moving forward by leaps and bounds. Why shouldn't we get access to the technologies of the future in only a few years' time? Can the present generations break out from mass confusion and hyperthink and conquer the future? Or will we succumb to our inability to make sense of the confusing development that is going on and see through the veil of misconception? We are likely to get the answer in the coming decade.

7

How Technology and System Development Work

It is important to build a picture in our minds of the large-scale development programs that need to get started and the understanding of the organized activities that must form the foundation of such endeavors.

The psychologists quoted earlier noted that people tend to forget information that goes contrary to their beliefs that have been built over decades. Some clear examples are likely to bring insight and clarity to our confused thoughts.

Technology Development and Economic Growth

Technology and system development are complex processes that run across decades and centuries, all the time building on existing technologies and previous results, taking development and implementation step-by-step toward more advanced applications and increasingly competitive system solutions. The Apollo program and the other successful initiatives described in this book are examples indicating that it is possible to achieve very ambitious goals, provided that relevant financing is offered and that stringent management principles are applied.

But these start-up programs only developed the first generation of technologies. To develop the second, third, and fourth generations, large-scale government investment needs to continue in combination with large-scale financing from private sources. This is because the first generation of any technology is seldom competitive enough for growth to take off based on financing from market-based players. In the case of computers, it took until the first years of the twenty-first century, more than fifty years after the first computer, for the development of IT to contribute to economic growth.

Before that, economists were confused by the so-called "IT paradox." Despite the increasing use of computers for many different purposes, Nobel Prize Laureate Robert Solow observed in 1987: "You can see the computer age everywhere but in the productivity statistics." Government investment in the development of computers and the ARPANET contributed substantially to reducing the time it took for the technologies to start to contribute to economic growth. Still, it took a very long time. Without such investments, it is likely to take a similarly long time to drive electromobility and other important technologies to maturity.

The management principles applied in successful projects are examples of principles that are known to work. What we can deduce is that it will be much less likely that a random set of activities will lead to a particular outcome. When the systems that are to be developed have not been carefully designed, and when there is no one involved to make sure that all the necessary development steps and activities are undertaken, it is highly unlikely that the result will be what people expect.

It is a telling example that one reason why quality control systems, like the ISO 9001 standard, were developed is that the US Army gave multiple companies the assignment to make gasoline cans and received cans from different suppliers that were inconsistent in design, despite having sent the same drawings to all manufacturers. The army then realized that they had to first specify the design and then force suppliers to follow very strict manufacturing processes to make sure that they receive identical products.

That was when they were ordering relatively simple products like gasoline cans. When it comes to the development of entire systems for electromobility and to the change from petroleum-fueled transport systems, processes will have to be even more tightly managed. The same will have to be true for the other development processes mentioned in this book.

If very large amounts of money are invested in more or less random technology development, even if the best brains are applied to evaluate project applications and coordinate individual projects, it will still be unlikely that the overall development will be successful and that large-scale and competitive systems for, for example, electromobility, will emerge through the process.

The trends are similar across the world. A number of successful examples of technology and business development from the past have been mentioned. American governments have contributed to the development of many important technologies. The same has been the case in Europe, where government-owned companies and agencies have built power systems, landline and mobile phone networks, railways, and many other facilities that make modern life comfortable and efficient.

Suddenly, in the early years of the twenty-first century, governments, companies, and citizens start to believe that tremendous advances can be made without building knowledge about the challenges at hand, and without managing innovation and development processes.

In the final analysis in his 2005 book, *Is War Necessary for Economic Growth?*, Ruttan concluded that war may not be necessary for economic growth, but the fear of war may be necessary to mobilize the resources needed for the large-scale and long-term financing that will be required to take technologies from early stages of development to fully fledged mature technologies.

In development programs, especially the ones with a tight deadline and expectations of a very specific outcome, stringent management and large-scale and long-term government financing will be needed. Not only will it be necessary to build an understanding of the technical challenges, but a variety of management principles and financing mechanisms need to be applied in different situations, which makes it necessary to build knowledge in these areas.

The Development of Airplane Technologies

Many readers are likely to doubt that large public investment will be needed for new technologies to reach maturity, but earlier processes clearly indicate that this has always been the case, and we can safely assume that the same will be needed in the future as well. In the early stages, it has been necessary for governments to drive the process forward through long-term and large-scale investment. It has not been until technologies have approached maturity that private investment and the market can take over as the most important sources of financing, but even at this stage, governments, in many cases, have continued to invest, long after technologies have become general-purpose.

In the past decades, air travel has become increasingly inexpensive, and the market has, to a large extent, driven the expansion of commercial air travel, but government investment still plays an important role in technology development and improvement. For example, governments invest in the development of military aircraft that spills over into civil aviation. Large-scale financing is also provided for the development of passenger aircraft as European and US governments try to make sure that the competing market leaders Boeing and Airbus keep their positions.

In the early stages, governments drove development for decades, almost single-handedly, making investments and offering subsidies without which air travel and transportation would not have been able to reach its present level of development. But it should be noted that some initiatives turn out to be dead ends. The development of the ultrasonic passenger aircraft Concorde, driven as a collaborative project between France and the United Kingdom, did not get any followers. A total of twenty aircraft were built and kept in service from 1976 to 2003, but despite this and other costly detours, air travel has become one of the highly successful technologies of our modern society that has contributed significantly to economic growth.

From the early days of the twentieth century, the US government used three principal tools to drive development in the airline industry: heavy subsidies for airmail, the procurement of military aircraft, and the financing of research and development programs.

As early as 1915, the government established NACA, the National Advisory Committee for Aeronautics, and the aircraft industry became the only manufacturing industry that had a government research organization with the sole purpose of supporting the industry's research and development.

As the United States entered the First World War, its European allies demanded that they increase the production of aircraft. In 1916 only 411 airplanes were produced, but the industry, with only 300 companies, expanded to 175,000 workers who between April 1917 and November 1918 produced 12,894 aircraft and 41,983 engines. By the end of the war, the engines had become stronger, but no major breakthroughs had been made in the design. At the time, primarily military planes were produced, but in 1918, an airmail service was opened between New York and Washington, DC. In 1925, the introduction of rotating beacons at airports made night flight possible, and by 1930, a transcontinental system had been established.

Companies were started with the purpose of handling mail transportation, and the services were subsidized to become profitable. Companies were paid by the volume of the aircraft, which created an incentive to also make room for a few passengers. As Herbert Hoover became postmaster general, he moved to promote mergers between airlines to create regional and national carriers and increase the efficiency of the industry. This was done with the intention of building a modern aircraft industry and a national system for air transport. By 1933, four major airlines (American, TWA, Eastern, and United) were in operation, and this structure remained until after the Second World War.

In its first ten years of operation, NACA focused on two major tasks, propeller design and the construction of advanced wind tunnels. In the coming decades, research was funded to investigate the interaction between the pilot and the plane and to develop more efficient engines. The NACA facility at Langley Field was recognized in the 1930s as the leading aviation research center in the world.

In 1913, US investment in the aircraft industry was on par with that of Brazil, while the leaders Germany and France invested more than fifty times that amount. In 1939, the United States built the best commercial airliners and the country had the largest airline system in the world. The DC3 airplane, launched in the 1930s and remaining in operation until the 1960s, incorporated technologies that had been developed for military aircraft and engines.

NACA management was not convinced of the necessity to develop jet propulsion, since it required new aerody- namics for flight and these technologies were not available in the US. Instead, German and British engineers and companies took the lead in this development.

Boeing developed a military jet, the B47, containing revolutionary technology that was also applied in the production of its first commercial jet airliner, the 707. The ability to apply technology that had been developed in military projects to the development of commercial airliners constitutes an important basis for Boeing's success.

After the Second World War, the aircraft industry was the United States' largest industry. Large public investment had gone into the development and purchase of military aircraft. For example, 13,726 B17 bombers had been built during the war, and the number of fighters was much higher. The total number of aircraft built by the United States in the war was 296,600,[17] and Boeing had established itself as a leading manufacturer of military aircraft and could transfer that position to become the leader in the commercial airliner industry.

In the 1930s, NACA embarked on a program to develop high-speed flight, which culminated with the first supersonic flight in 1947.

In 1958, NASA was founded and NACA was incorporated into the new organization. The driving forces of the US Air Force's transition to jet propulsion and the need to continue to develop high-speed aviation technologies kept research and development at a high level. Investments in R&D amounted to 20 percent of gross revenue in the

---

17   The number of aircraft can be found on page 353 of *An Empire of Wealth* by John Steele Gordon.

aircraft industry, of which only a tenth (2 percent) was financed through private sources.

In the 1980s, the United States' commercial aircraft industry faced strong competition from European manufacturers, which led the US government to invest one billion dollars per year on an ongoing basis in all aspects of commercial aircraft development and demonstration. In his reflections, Ruttan concludes that the industry could not have developed in the way it has without the long-term and large-scale government investments that have been made since 1915.[18]

Investment in the development of new technologies and new industrial sectors must be made by governments because they are made with a time horizon from investment to payback that cannot be handled by private companies. The primary drivers of the development of the aircraft industry were the growth of the country's infrastructure and military strength. Building the competitive position of the aircraft industry has been an important aspect as well, but probably not as important as the first two priorities, Ruttan concludes. Private investment needs to pay back in only a few years. In the cases studied, the US government had invested billions of dollars over seven decades, without the expectation for the investments to pay back short term. In many cases, it has been uncertain if the investments would ever pay back.

The book's title, *Is War Necessary for Economic Growth?*,

---

18 The full analysis is available on pages 33-65 of *Is War Necessary for Economic Growth?* by Vernon W. Ruttan.

refers to the strategic aspect of the investments made by the US government and the possibility that large-scale and long-term financing cannot be mustered in the absence of a military threat. In the absence of such funding, Ruttan concludes, there is a substantial risk that economic growth will come to a halt.

The growth that has been enjoyed in the world in the past century seems, to a large extent, to be a by-product of strategic investments and not something that has been created primarily for financial or commercial reasons. The focused programs and financial backing from governments have been important drivers of innovation, and technology upon technology has been developed and has proliferated to deliver cost-effective applications in many areas. Politicians and economists, specializing in policy development, have turned a blind eye to the role of governments in this respect, a blindness that has created a large territory of ignorance and a culture of mass confusion and hyperthink throughout society.

Other Examples of Technology Development

The development of space and computer technologies and the internet have been financed by the government in similar ways, and the same is true for the American production system, which was developed in the nineteenth century. In the case of nuclear power, Ruttan concludes that this technology would probably never even have come into existence in the absence of government investment.

In the case of the auto industry, which is not discussed by Ruttan, growth and development took off as countries started to motorize their armies and needed large numbers of identical vehicles that were reliable and easy to repair and maintain. This, in combination with the development of the assembly line by Henry Ford, drove down the price of cars so that the demand for cars could increase to present levels, but it was still not until after the Second World War that the majority of households in developed countries could afford to buy one.

Conclusions for the Future

Based on his studies, Ruttan, at the start of the new millennium, concluded that the private sector would not drive the development of new general-purpose technologies. He also thought it doubtful whether governments would have the incentive to invest large enough sums in the development of non-military technologies and that new general-purpose technologies may not be developed in the future.[19]

Without a doubt, many of the technologies that have driven growth in the past decades approach full penetration of the largest markets; the lack of obvious

---

19 Ruttan discussed the prospects for new general-purpose technologies on pages 177-185.

new candidates that can drive future growth should be cause for concern. Ruttan could not observe the formation of the type of large-scale programs he deemed necessary to rapidly drive the technologies of the future to maturity.

The investments that have been described above represent a magnitude and duration that most experts on specific technologies are not likely to be aware of. It will require substantial research to define the status of development of candidate technologies today, such as electro-mobility, artificial intelligence, autonomous vehicles, and new materials, and determine the amount of investment that will be necessary for large-scale implementation to take place.

Other Views of the Future of Technology Development

Economic and technological development is much more complex than most students of the future realize. When reading *The Inevitable,* by Kevin Kelly, *The Future is Faster Than You Think,* by Peter Diamandis and Steven Kotler, and other similar visions of the future, the reader is given the impression that many aspects of the development are certain and unquestionable. Kelly argues that digital technologies will continue to be developed at a pace that will move society forward to the point where artificial intelligence, robotics, and other technologies will become inexpensive general-purpose technologies.

The process he describes as inevitable can only take place in a society with significant economic growth. It will be important to determine if growth can continue for much longer and stake out a strategy for development that can sustain a high pace. There is a significant risk that this will not be the case and that society will come up against unexpected challenges that have up until now been neglected.

Efficiency Improvements and Value Creation

The reason why economic growth may be at risk is that it depends on efficiency improvements and continuous value creation. Efficiency improvements arise because the time and cost of performing activities are reduced significantly. An increasing number of tasks are now performed in almost no time and at a cost close to zero. This creates a situation in which it becomes more difficult to further reduce costs, and the value of future improvements is likely to be lower than that of improvements made earlier in the process.

Early in a development, when tasks were manual, markets were local or national, and little attention had been paid to efficiency improvement, large leaps were possible. As development has been going on for decades, much of the cost and time has been eliminated from business processes and from tasks at home, such as dishwashing and cleaning, which have also become more efficient over the past one hundred years.

For example, computer transactions are performed with high precision almost instantly and at a very low cost. By using computers, the time used to perform tasks that took significant time only ten or twenty years ago, like writing a letter or a report, has been reduced significantly, and it has become questionable whether such tasks can be made much more efficient.

One further example is Google searches, which in a fraction of a second manage to find all the documents on the internet covering the subject searched for. Google also orders the hits so that the most relevant pieces of information top the listing.

Bookkeeping is another example. It was, for a long time, done manually in ledgers. Now, most accounting is done automatically, and at a time and cost close to zero, as transactions are made.

Improvement methods, like Lean Management, developed by Toyota after the Second World War, have been used for decades across the world to reduce the time and cost of business processes. Now, many companies have nearly eliminated the waste of time and other resources and also greatly reduced the time needed to add value to products and services. When only a little time remains, the savings opportunities are not as big as they were at the beginning of the improvement process, so the value of each new saving is on average much smaller than with earlier improvements.

The opportunity to add more value still exists, but value creation is also limited in many cases. Mobile phones offered significant new value. Suddenly, time that used to be wasted could be used for valuable business calls or chats with friends. Now, this value has been captured and an increasing share of communication is done in the form of emails and text messages, which has improved efficiency even further.

The access to washing machines and dishwashers has also added significant value and quality of life to people. Now that we have washing machines and many households have two dishwashers, which allows families to reduce the time used for emptying the machines, this value has been captured as well.

Companies, entrepreneurs, and innovators have worked intensely for the past century to identify areas where new value can be created. Many opportunities have been exploited and products and services have been developed that have helped capture value and integrate it into the economy. It is uncertain how much additional value remains to be created in the future, but it seems likely that the potential for value creation, just as the potential for improving efficiency, is not infinite.

When Do Technologies Become General-Purpose?

It is not until a technology becomes inexpensive and is used by companies and people for many purposes that it becomes a general-purpose technology. It is about that time when it starts to contribute to economic growth. The reason for this is straightforward. Large savings are achieved when many users get access to new technologies and take the opportunity to reduce time and cost at work or in their private lives.

When a technology matures, even though lower-level savings may continue for many decades, it is only for a short period of time that it contributes significantly to economic growth. The reason for this is also straight-forward. Economic growth is a measurement of the *increase* of the value created compared to the previous year, the growth of GDP. During a period when a rapidly increasing number of people get access to a technology, productivity improvement is likely to be significant. When most people already use the technology, efficiency improvement decreases. At this point, the price of the technology may still go down and the efficiency is likely to continue to improve due to continuous development and increasing use. This creates room for people to spend money on other things, but savings are no longer big enough for society to outweigh the investment.

A somewhat spooky aspect of this is that society can never reach a high enough level of affluence. New improvements in productivity still need to be made every year for economic growth to continue and for people to be able to continue to enjoy their present level of prosperity.

We need to collectively run faster all the time even to keep our present level of development.

Still, it deserves to be repeated that incremental improvement will not be enough to drive economic growth and develop the society of the future. Breakthroughs in new areas will be necessary to create the means to invest in the progress people expect.

In principle, the advances that were made in the previous year became irrelevant on the 31st of December when the productivity improvements for the present year started. The level of GDP per capita that has been achieved in a sense indicates the level of affluence, but the level is not absolute. Affluence can only be maintained through continuous growth, and inflation can quickly erode progress.

If citizens believe that economic growth will decline in the long term, affluence is likely to start to decline as well. These aspects are well-known, but they are seldom taken into consideration by sustainability experts when they discuss the transformation to a sustainable society. If experts and decision-makers had been aware of how building the future really works, the highly simplified ideas, such as that the market will be able to drive change, would not have gained the level of traction that they have and contributed to the mass confusion of the present.

It has taken me twenty-five years to arrive at some of these insights, and I have actively been searching for and verifying the ideas that make up the reasoning of this book.

I have meticulously followed different trains of thought to their logical conclusion. For example, the adoption of electromobility may be an important innovation that causes emissions of carbon dioxide to go down, but for the economy, it adds time for charging to the time already taken by driving, and for some routes the use of electric trucks may cause an increase in the number of vehicles needed by 30 percent. Electric road networks will probably be needed to bring transportation by electric vehicle up to the present level of efficiency of fossil-fuel trucks, buses, and cars. On top of the loss of efficiency due to the need for stationary charging comes the higher price of electric vehicles. It is not until the past few years that I have found research that supports my assumption that electric roads are likely to become necessary to make electric vehicle systems efficient. Companies that develop these technologies, like Elonroad in Sweden, and university professors that lead research initiatives try to inform the public about the necessity to build extensive networks.

The change to electric vehicles will be necessary, but it has to be done swiftly to maintain the efficiency of transportation, which is an important reason behind the efficiency of the present global economy. It is equally important to invest in power production and grids and make sure that sufficient power will be available at competitive prices to make it possible to convert transport systems and build up the manufacturing resources and other systems that will be needed in the future.

The examples illustrate the investment needs in the development of technologies for them to contribute to economic growth. Very large investment needs to be made over the long term and to achieve this governments need determination and focus, in the way that governments had in the past when they invested in railways, telephone networks, and space technologies.

Great technical advances are not likely to be achieved if a laissez-faire approach is taken and investment in the development of a technology is left to the market entirely. Surprisingly, and probably to a large extent without planning, governments and large companies in the twentieth century made investments that sixty or seventy years later have contributed to economic growth. They did this for decades, in some cases from the nineteenth century and for many decades into the twentieth.

An important additional observation is the number of technologies that have contributed to economic growth in the past decades. The technologies discussed above are not the only ones that have driven development. New materials, improved production technologies, automation, miniaturization, the development in the automotive sector, chemicals, and a number of other examples have together contributed to improving productivity. It deserves to be repeated that the present generations run the risk of finding that very few, or perhaps no, new technologies have come far enough toward maturity to drive economic growth in the coming decades.

As the power of existing mature technologies starts to wane, it is likely to be difficult to once more drive growth in the global economy. These are only some of the aspects to which economists, sustainability experts, and governments have become blind, and the price of this blindness will be paid by the citizens of nations across the world. This blindness has extended to transnational organizations like the UN and the EU, and it has further contributed to the difficulty of putting a halt to hyperthink and getting public discourse onto a more constructive route. The blindness has made it impossible to explore the territories of ignorance and discuss findings.

Many people tend to think that government investment in technology development and implementation belong to left-wing politics only, but it has been one of the bulwarks that have built and strengthened platforms for market-based development for over one hundred years.

Necessary Development Initiatives

Some development initiatives are more important than others. There are systems in society that are so critical that governments need to go out of their way to make sure that they will continue to work and that they will remain as efficient as they are today, and even more, if possible. Europe has already experienced what happens when there are disturbances in power production due to reduced supplies of natural gas from Russia and when there is not enough production from other energy sources to cover the loss.

In the case of electromobility, vehicle owners may replace vehicles with electric alternatives, but without enough electricity, it will be impossible to expand fleets rapidly enough to maintain the capacity of transport systems. A large share of electric vehicle fleets may be rendered immobile at times when electricity gets scarce. The development of electricity generation needs to be done in ways that both provide a stable volume of supply at all times when substantial amounts of power are needed and balance the grids to eliminate the risk of large-scale breakdowns. Different generation technologies offer different production profiles, and they do not provide the same stability to balance grids.

There are many different types of risks that may pose a threat to transportation in case development is not synchronized:

- Disturbances to the power supply through a reduced supply of fuel or a protracted wind lull can cause shortages and price hikes.
- The price of electricity may remain high for long periods of time and cause companies to go bankrupt or make electric transportation and other uses of electricity unprofitable and unviable.
- A large focus on the promotion of electric vehicles is likely to drive machining companies that make parts for combustion engines out of business because

very little demand for the machining of parts will arise from the transformation to electric vehicles. When the sales of electric vehicles start to take over on a large scale, measures will be needed to retrain workers for new jobs and manage the large-scale and rapid move from the machining of parts to a large-scale increase in the production of electric motors and batteries. But overall, each electric car requires fewer hours in production compared to a gasoline car. Instead, a need to expand charging infrastructure and power grids will create many job opportunities but also a demand for people with skills in these areas.

- If it then turns out that there is not enough electricity to fuel electric vehicles, it may be both difficult and costly to go back to producing gasoline and diesel vehicles. Fossil-fuel vehicles need to be phased out at a speed that can be supported by all participants in the transformation.

To maintain the efficiency of transport systems, electric vehicles also need to rapidly become less expensive. The reduction of the cost of air travel has to a large extent arisen from the large-scale funding of the development of airplane technologies by governments. It is likely that similar large-scale and long-term financing programs will be needed for battery technologies, electric road systems, and the various other technologies that will be necessary for the development and expansion of autonomous vehicles.

Each Development — Specific Needs

I started researching the conversion to electromobility in 2004; I have also researched other changes, among them the multitude that will be needed to create a circular and sustainable economy. During the better part of the time since, very little has happened in terms of large-scale change.

The release of the Tesla Roadster in 2008 sped up the growth of electromobility. Until Tesla came on the scene, most car makers had developed electric cars as defensive measures in case the development would take off. There was no sign of any intention to drive the development forward at high speed. The first generations of electric cars only offered a relatively short range, in the area of seventy miles, and few realized that it would be possible to build affordable battery packs that could offer four or five times that distance.

Despite the large focus on the implementation of electric vehicles, only 3–4 percent of all cars in most countries are electric and no country has yet experienced a situation in which a large share is electric. The first models of electric trucks have been launched over the past few years, and the share of electric transport vehicles is still very low. As has been argued in the text, very little attention has been paid to the change process, which is also a reason why the change has not come further by now, despite the insistent arguments by sustainability experts that more resources need to be invested by governments and private companies in the creation of a sustainable society.

At present, the situation regarding a circular and sustainable economy is similar to how it was in the earliest days of electromobility. Many actors pay lip service to the intention to change the global economy to sustainable flows, but neither politicians, business leaders, nor experts do anything significant to make the change happen. In Sweden, one of the measures has been to implement a tax on plastic bags to reduce the number used. Unfortunately, it has been shown that plastic bags are the most environmentally friendly bags, much better than textile bags that require more resources in production, primarily water for growing cotton. Now, many politicians are considering repealing the law.

During my work with my first projects in the area of the circular economy, I identified about a dozen companies in Sweden that applied circular business models and that I used as case studies in my report and in the subsequent book *Circular Business Models.* Despite the great interest in the circular economy, very little has happened since 2016 in terms of volume growth or new breakthrough innovations, and few new examples of companies with circular business models have been added that have become successful enough to receive publicity.

From 2019 to 2021, I was one of two managers of a project aimed at helping Swedish municipalities purchase more products and services with circular properties. Doing this turned out to be very difficult due to the small number of circular products and services available and the high prices of those that exist. The high prices are primarily due to the small volumes in which these products are made and sold and the undeveloped supply chains of the companies involved in this type of production. Despite high hopes, there is a big risk that the development of a circular economy will be very slow as there are few products and services that are competitive against incumbent alternatives. It is in fact likely that the volumes of circular and sustainable alternatives are still declining, continuing the process that has been going on for decades.

A change to autonomous vehicles will need entirely different types of measures compared to the change to biological plastics, which is one of the concepts under the umbrella of the circular economy. For autonomous vehicles to become a reality, governments and companies need to find ways to surpass the promises of Moore's Law and dramatically increase the capacity for communication between vehicles and the cloud.

To turn the promises of the different aspects of the circular economy into reality and speed up the creation of a sustainable society, specific measures will be needed, aimed at expanding the use of the different principles under the umbrella of the circular economy:

- To replace fossil plastics with renewable plastics, many more fossil-free materials need to be made available. This is a particular challenge as the amounts of oil used to produce plastics are vast and the amount of biological raw materials available for plastics production is much smaller.

- To change the food supply from national and global production systems to an increasing share of locally produced food will require the development of new ecosystems of companies that collaborate around local food production and distribution. The amount of food produced by such firms is very small at present.

- To get people to engage in sharing schemes and share vehicles, tools, and other resources between households and in society at large, people need information about the logic of doing this, and more sharing services need to be established with a cost profile that can make these services affordable.

There are many hurdles, except the price of products and services that need to be removed to turn the above technologies into large-scale successes. It may be the case that some of the ideas will be difficult or impossible to implement on a large scale, due to factors such as the time it takes for people to pick up and return tools and other products that have been rented or borrowed from sharing services. This is likely to reduce the demand for such services, and other business models may need to be developed instead.

Like the beacons that were installed in the United States in 1925 to make night flight possible, research needs not only to develop the technologies and services themselves but also to investigate what will be needed to succeed. This will allow the removal of other obstacles and the setting of realistic goals for the savings potential of various ideas. Concepts with limited potential will need less financing than ones with a large potential for resource savings and reduction of emissions.

Development Programs and Competence Development

It seems as if the conclusion that change needs to be managed cannot be widely discussed, perhaps because it is not seen as politically correct to put it forward. There is also a lack of knowledge about the history of technology development and the large-scale programs that have been important drivers in the past. The opportunity to discuss ideas may open up once more when people see the need for structured activities to develop and implement the new systems. After all, many governments subsidize electric cars and charging posts, and a host of other needs for government funding appear on the horizon.

In a similar way, other development initiatives that

need to be started to develop a sustainable society are supported on a small scale and without coordination. The result is that this support has little effect. Development is, in many areas, almost at a standstill. Many people are confused. How could it be that governments have announced plans to develop a sustainable society, but so little happens in the way of creating it? Governments need to take the initiative of investigating the entire investment needed to go through with the changes discussed here.

Few people understand that no country has access to the competence needed to drive the change forward. The situation is like the one that existed in the field of space exploration before the Apollo program. Very few people had studied what would be required to send a man to the moon and bring him safely back to Earth. John F. Kennedy realized this and gave NASA a generous budget that kickstarted space travel and built up an entire space technology sector in the United States. During the program four hundred thousand Americans were engaged. The program also kickstarted the development of the space industry and the four hundred thousand people became well organized so that they could contribute productively to the development.

In the cases of electromobility, autonomous vehicles, and the change to a sustainable society, governments, sustainability experts, and companies are stuck with ideas that have never been put to the test on any significant scale.

Governments need to organize change. Otherwise, hyperthink will continue to prevail and mass confusion will spread even further. In the absence of systematic and organized activities, the entropy of thought will continue in society and people will become even more confused as to how the large challenges ahead will be mastered. Mass confusion will tighten its grip over society and, despite some funding of individual projects, very little will be achieved.

8
Organizing Change

Development and change programs need to be well organized and generously financed. They are the activities that have the potential to create the future. Both large-scale public and private investment will be necessary, but private investment will, for a long time, remain very risky in the absence of large-scale public funding. Some companies manage to identify opportunities to achieve rapid results, often referred to as *low-hanging fruit,* and develop products and services that address low-risk business opportunities that can be realized with limited investment, but large-scale change will require large-scale and long-term financing.

Analyses of the risk of different solutions and system configurations need to be made, and countries need to collaborate to develop stable systems and new technologies on a large scale.

Organized Competence Needed

Development increases complexity in society by continuously adding new technologies, ideas, and tools that can be used for different purposes. This process has, for centuries, contributed to economic growth and improved affluence. But at the same time, it increases the alternative technologies and ideas that can be developed and the number of alternative routes of development that are possible to embark on. It also makes it more difficult for decision-makers and experts to focus enough resources on the most important alternatives or complexes of technologies, systems, and organizational solutions that need to be developed.

The post-war period was a situation when it, due to two world wars and the subsequent Cold War, was less complicated to funnel resources into highly prioritized projects. National security and economic growth were at the top of people's minds, and governments made efforts to speed up relevant development.

In a world with an increasing number of alternatives, it becomes even more important for governments to concentrate resources in the most important areas. However, complexity also drives the creation of more groups in society with agendas to support each of the new ideas developed. All want governments to support their favorite technologies and ideas, and it becomes politically dangerous to fund some development alternatives at the

expense of others. Complexity fuels the further proliferation of technologies and views, which in its turn increases
complexity even further.

Many and Complex Issues

For the issues that have been discussed in this book,
even many of the people who seemingly have spent time
penetrating them have come to questionable conclusions.
Or more to the point, many have not taken reasoning to
its logical conclusion. This is often the result when issues
are approached from only one perspective and people
with other perspectives are banned from participating in
discussions.

For example, when countries expand power generation from wind and solar on a large scale, it is critical to
secure access to backup resources of plannable generation
technologies that can be used to balance grids and secure
the supply of enough electricity to cover periods of wind
lull and that are able to generate at night when there is no
sun. Most experts should know this, but these measures
have still not been taken into consideration when systems
of wind turbines and solar cells have been expanded, as
has for example been done in Germany and Denmark.

I spoke to one professor, who has been involved in
various aspects of the construction of nuclear reactors,
who admitted that he had only in the past few years understood that different generation technologies offer entirely

different opportunities to balance power grids and create a stable supply of electricity. Wind and solar power can work well for the supply of power for the lighting of cities and other less demanding applications. To provide a stable power supply to heavy industry, generation technologies with heavy turbines are needed, such as nuclear power, hydroelectric, or fossil-fuel generation technologies.

It seems logical to rely on energy sources that can be controlled by countries themselves or spread risk between different sources to make sure that a breakdown in the relations with one supplier, like Russia, or an extended wind lull during one or two months, will not bring down the power supply of an entire continent.

This is admittedly difficult, because in the fall of 2022, twenty-six out of France's fifty-six nuclear reactors stood still, production from a large number of wind turbines, primarily in Germany, was low, due to low wind, and Europe's supply of gas had taken a beating due to Russia's invasion of Ukraine. How can individual countries, or the EU for that matter, secure themselves against this number of converging disasters? It was perhaps a very unlikely situation, but one that, if it would continue for several years, could threaten economic growth and affluence in Europe and potentially in the world at large.

Nevertheless, even for very complex issues there are more stable and less risky solutions and there are ones that increase the likelihood of disaster. Governments need to cooperate and develop structures that reduce the risk of power shortages to a minimum and make sure that possible shortages of power and capacity are as brief as possible and that they can be made to pass without doing significant harm to economies or to the affluence of people.

This type of consideration is made, for example, when countries build up their military. To defend their land and keep potential enemies from attacking, they need a certain size and configuration of military resources in the form of an army, a navy with enough resources to defend against attacks from the sea, and an air force with a similar power to defend against air strikes.

Even though it is difficult to configure and build these resources and arrive at a situation that provides a reasonable level of security, countries manage to do this. Even if the navy commander argues in favor of increasing the size of the navy, nobody, not even the commander himself, would argue that the government should invest all its money in the navy and entirely dismantle the air force and the army.

One of the factors that is decisive in the ability of countries to do these types of analyses is the availability of orgware. Governments need access to organized competence, not only to think tanks and university professors with diverging ideas. In well-structured organizations built for the purpose of driving development and change, experts and researchers have built up the ability to analyze issues from all relevant perspectives, and experts on specific issues still have the understanding necessary to also consider the systemic implications.

Based on an analysis of different scenarios, the most important investments are prioritized, and a reasonably well-balanced military is developed. Is a similar way of organizing development applicable to the structuring of energy systems, electromobility, autonomous vehicles, and the development of a sustainable economy at large?

Political Correctness and Shadow Science

In 2021, the Tesla Club Sweden, in an article on their website, simply extrapolated the increase in the sales of electric cars in the country and argued that the last fossil-fuel car may be sold in Sweden in 2026.[20] The article says that the exact date cannot be determined, but it still seems as if the club believed that the method could be used to forecast the end of the sales of fossil-fuel cars, even though the share of electric and hybrid cars was less than 5 percent.

At the time I read a number of newspaper articles that picked up the idea and argued that the last gasoline or diesel car would be sold in only a few years, suggesting, for example, 2028. None of these had looked at any other aspect of the development than the increase in sales up until 2021.

Expressing   optimism   about   the   growth   of

---

20 https://teslaclubsweden.se/sista-avgasbilen-i-sverige-saljs-redan-nasta-ar/.

electromobility was clearly a politically correct thing to do, and nobody seemed to question either the relevance of the approach or the forecast. Optimism is contagious, and nobody seemed to want to break the spell. It is theoretically possible that all cars sold in Sweden from 2026 or 2028 and onwards could be electric, but there are many factors that need to be considered to evaluate this prediction.

It is also questionable whether it would be advantageous for a country to drive the development at this speed, considering that no analyses have been made of the competitiveness of an economy with only electric cars in a global market where most countries still rely on more cost-effective technologies. Rapidly adopting a significantly more expensive transportation alternative is likely to adversely affect the competitiveness of the economy and create a multitude of risks, especially if it turns out that there will not be enough electricity to supply the growing vehicle fleets with electricity at competitive prices. It goes without saying that being one of the leading countries in a global development opens up many business opportunities, but it is important to also consider the risks.

When the articles were published that proclaimed the end of the sales of fossil-fuel cars before 2030, I tried to argue that the change would be more complex, that significant investment would be needed, and that investments would involve the construction of new power plants, wind turbines, and solar panels and the reinforcement of power grids in hundreds of local areas that may take decades. I admitted that the challenges for Sweden would be smaller than those of other countries, due to the very large amount of electricity per person that is produced here. Sweden has twice the amount of electricity available per person compared to Germany, and three times the amount of the UK. Per capita electricity generation in Sweden is on par with that of the United States.

My activities could be described as a type of shadow science, a line of reasoning that most people I talked to seemed to understand would become necessary, but that few people really wanted or dared to discuss. A case in point would be a discussion I had with an author from Finland, a businessperson, who had written a book with the title *One Planet is Enough*, in which he argued that the fear that the resources of the Earth would not suffice was exaggerated. He argued that miniaturization and improved energy efficiency would solve the problem and that nobody would have to worry about resource depletion. The author had apparently not investigated the availability of resources, nor the rate of use, or, for example, the *energy paradox*, the fact that despite measures to save energy since the 1970s, demand has increased faster than energy has been saved. The book was first published in Swedish, the author's native language.

We met at a book exhibition, and I argued that, despite energy efficiency and miniaturization, an increasing amount of both energy and materials are used and that the supply of some resources may start to decline over the next decade or two. For example, oil consumption is increasing by between 1 and 2 percent every year, despite efforts to reduce its use, and this increase will continue for a number of years, despite the growth of electric vehicles. Each year more than thirty-one billion barrels of oil are used. If barrels would be stacked on top of each other, it would take less than five days for the stack to reach the moon. This would be less time than it took for Apollo 11 to go the same distance.

At the same time, fewer new oil reserves are found every year. Less than 10 percent of the annual consumption is discovered in the form of new wells. I told him that, according to the analyses of oil industry experts, the peak in oil production would be reached sooner than most people are aware of, and in the years following the peak, oil production would decline and it would not be likely to recover. Thus, it was not only because of emissions of carbon dioxide and global warming that the use of oil would have to be cut.

I also argued that it will be necessary to secure access to transportation in the future. With the increasing production of shale oil and other types of unconventional oil, production is still increasing, but it would be unlikely for shale oil to take over all oil production when the decline of the production of conventional oil speeds up. Governments would have to start programs to reduce dependence on oil and implement electromobility on a large scale.

The author nodded and said that he understood. He said that if there is a limited supply and this supply would run out, his argument could not hold. He also admitted that if miniaturization would not affect the use of resources, such as steel and concrete that are used for buildings, vehicles, and other things that are not subject to miniaturization, the argument would not hold either.

Despite this, he continued his argumentation after the exhibition, and a few years later I noticed that his book had been published in an English edition as well. The example, although it is of little importance for the development on a global scale, illustrates the forces at play. Even if arguments are untenable, authors and experts are likely to continue to spread them. A lot of time and effort has been invested in the writing of books and the development of arguments and people are likely to believe what they read or hear. If messages are optimistic and seem politically correct, people are bound to continue to believe in them and pass them on.

To stop the process, a paradigm shift will be needed, and people will have to be trained in the various disciplines that they will need to master to productively participate in large-scale change projects. This will have to involve the training of large numbers of people to grasp the details of the changes needed, in much the same way that companies train their employees in change management so that they can drive change in corporations. For example, companies like General Electric and IBM have reinvented themselves over and over again in the past decades.

In this book, many different and conflicting views are brought up. Teams of experts and decision-makers need to take on the task of developing a holistic picture of the future and stake out a route forward that balances risks and opportunities and that also takes into account the pressing need to develop sustainable production, distribution, and transport systems.

The hidden shadow science needs to be brought out in the open and replace the simplistic and overly optimistic claims made by sustainability experts and businesspersons who approach the topic only from one perspective. More people need to understand that adding more infantry soldiers with rifles will not be sufficient to expand a country's military strength or take up the equivalent reasoning for the developments discussed in this book.

It is not necessarily difficult to do this. It has been achieved in many areas, not only in military strategy. There is well-rounded competence in health care and many areas of technology and social sciences. Competence and organizational resources make it possible to drive development with an eye on all the relevant aspects at one and the same time.

The trick is to inform and train large numbers of people at the same time. When companies send single individuals to training courses, they come back to their colleagues who have not attended the course. The knowledge that has been acquired by the single individual rapidly becomes forgotten as colleagues continue to work as they have always done. In large change programs entire departments, or entire business units or companies, are trained to develop new ways of working. Even with this type of measure, change is difficult, but at least it becomes possible. Without broad training programs large-scale concerted change is almost impossible.

When David Lundberg and I wrote *The Transparent Market*, and when it was published in 1998, other experts on the internet and electronic business primarily took a technical perspective and predicted the development of e-business based on the current rate of growth. Many believed that all trade would soon be done on open internet platforms and that the incumbents at the time would see their market share dwindle and lose out to fast-growing companies like Amazon.

David and I took the perspective of business strategy and based our arguments on investment needs and the existing position of incumbents and argued that the development would be much more complex and that leaders in many industries would be able to defend their positions and develop winning strategies on the electronic market as well.

It turned out that we were right and that in most industries the development has not been a linear growth of open platforms for internet business with a maximum competition. The forecast of plummeting prices due to the lower transaction cost on the internet has also not turned into reality in most industries.

Even if a more thorough analysis of the arguments at the time and the development that has been going on since 1998 would be needed to drive home the point, the example illustrates the need to consider all relevant perspectives to forecast the future.

Leaders With Integrity

How can the present situation of mass confusion, hyperthink, and rampant, but unfounded, optimism be changed to a more balanced discussion of facts and developing realistic scenarios based on analysis and an understanding of the actual situation in each area?

Governments need to take on the role of leaders and finance change programs led by persons with strong integrity who use a structured and systematic approach to problem-solving, planning, and execution.

NASA had taken on the task of sending a man to the moon, and the organization could not embarrass itself by not delivering on its promises. In the same way, organizations have to be built with leaders who take their task seriously and recruit people with the same degree of integrity to work with the development.

Throughout the development programs, ideas and innovation needs must be balanced. All resources cannot be invested into the expansion of the infantry and the procurement of rifles.

In the same way, power systems cannot be built entirely on wind turbines and solar panels. There is also a definite need for plannable generation and technologies that can be used to balance power grids and for heavy-duty applications.

Understanding of Complex Processes, Not Static Facts

It is difficult to see how the situation could change over the coming years. Education at schools and universities is focused on teaching students static knowledge, or knowledge that changes very slowly, like history, geography, physics, language, and math. Mastering these skills is important, but much less time is spent understanding the dynamic processes of change that are going on at an increasing speed across the world today.

This knowledge includes how new technologies are developed and how products and systems developed on a small scale by individual companies come, decades later, to change the world and the way people live and work. To understand this and how this development is driven by economic growth and improvements in efficiency, an entirely different type of knowledge needs to be developed.

Many people have some of this knowledge, but only to a limited extent. A person may know a lot about ecology and how species fight for survival in their natural environment. Based on this understanding, they may draw conclusions about the need to change to a sustainable society, but they are likely to get many things wrong in terms of investment needs and the possible pace of change.

Young people may be able to learn impressive amounts of facts related to emissions and the warming of the planet, but they are not likely to grasp the processes that are at work when new technologies are developed and implemented on a large scale, or how entire industries need to be changed to facilitate the transformation to electromobility.

Perhaps a new profession of change leaders needs to be developed, consisting of people who can understand the dynamics of change in many different areas of society. In any case, conscious efforts need to be made to level up arguments from the present simplistic stage to a realistic understanding of the complexity involved in large-scale change.

Leading corporations have, over the past decades, gone through this process. In his 1992 book, *The New GE: How Jack Welch Revived an American Institution*, the former CEO of General Electric, Jack Welch, describes how he and his colleagues transformed the company from a slow-moving giant to an agile leader in its selected industries over the course of only a decade. Before the transformation, people at GE were good at their jobs, but they did not master the dynamics of change. After the transformation, the ability to change was built into the organization, and change has continued under the subsequent directors. GE has become not only a leader in the industries where it is active but a leader in the development of sustainable technologies.

The Big Question

When reviewing the arguments of the book, a big question emerges. The entropy of thought that results from it seems to be a law of nature.

With development over decades and centuries, complexity increases. Complexity makes it increasingly difficult to prioritize areas of development, focus resources, and make other tough decisions. The number of alternative solutions and routes forward increases almost exponentially, and it becomes more difficult to identify and prioritize the most important technologies, systems, and development activities.

With each year that goes by, it becomes more tempting to give up and say that it is not the task of any human decision-maker or body of decision-makers to steer development in the right direction. The market is instead seen as the best tool to do this, but this is impossible.

In this type of situation, will governments around the world be able to muster the resources and decision-making power to get their acts together, turn a blind eye to political correctness, stop the process of hyperthink, and lead development onto a productive path of rapid transformation of the most important industries and sectors of society?

It will be very interesting, but also daunting, to follow the development over the coming years.

Epilogue

Development and innovation are topics that are not easy to grasp. There are no off-the-shelf solutions that can be used by governments and experts to solve the problems of the present day. The situation now is completely different from how it used to be in the 1960s or the 1990s. Public debate and the development of political correctness have contributed to developing a multi-dimensional landscape of ideas and potential controversies that has to be navigated in the pursuit of workable solutions.

I have spent twenty-five years working out how building the future really works. The late Vernon Ruttan wrote the book I extensively refer to toward the end of his life. Professor Jan Blomgren, with whom I have been in dialogue over the past months, has arrived at some of his insights regarding generation technologies and the balancing of power grids in the past few years, after having worked with electricity systems for more than three decades. I do not blame people for not having come to the same insights, but it is important that many people take in these experiences and other similar learnings that will be important for the development of the future.

Once these insights have been developed, other people can more rapidly learn the same things, but knowledge may also rapidly dissipate into thin air if no one passes it on and continues to build on it.

The challenge that is facing the present generation is to make sense of the development and innovation landscape and find a way forward in an increasingly complex technical environment. This is no trivial task. The future of our technological society is at stake. If we fail to develop a strategy for the development, our children and grandchildren are not likely to experience the same level of affluence and prosperity that we enjoy at present. A much harsher future is then likely to emerge through a development that will be difficult or impossible to reverse.

This is a book where we follow thoughts to their logical conclusion. Anyone who doubts that large-scale and long-term government financing of innovation programs will have any significant impact on the speed of innovation could consider this:

What would the modern world have looked like without the government-financed programs of the past? It is unlikely that we would have had access to the type of computers and smartphones that we have, and GPS and other space-related technologies would probably not have been available in the way they are at present, without the Apollo program and subsequent space initiatives. It is also unlikely that we would have had access to nuclear power, cheap flights, and online shopping. Without space programs or with only market-based space development, miniaturization, lighter materials, and many other developments would probably not have come as far as they have.

Many other technologies have been developed or heavily promoted in programs financed by governments, and they have thus rapidly gone down in price and been developed to become more user-friendly. The price and operating cost of motor vehicles went down as armies became motorized. In Europe, railways, phone networks, and power grids were, to a large extent, developed through public-private cooperation, where public financing represented an important aspect behind their growth.

It seems unlikely that technology development will bring forward a large number of technical breakthroughs and new technologies and products in the absence of large-scale and long-term government financing in key areas.

Are we to continue to take an interest in our favorite topics, vote, and hope for the best, or should we start to learn more about the dynamics of technology development and change and help build the society of the future with all kinds of exciting new technologies? If the answer is the latter, the work needs to start now. More people need to start to break the spell of hyperthink, learn how to discuss development and change in constructive ways, and help bring their colleagues and friends out of mass confusion.

Together, we need to build a realistic vision of the future and start systematic development to create it. I would have liked to be able to describe in detail how it can be done, but just like neither John F. Kennedy, nor anyone else, could in detail describe the Apollo program in 1961, no person alive today can describe how we need to finance, organize, or create the change that lies ahead of humanity. We need to discover how the future can be conquered, and we need to embark on the journey, develop a strategy and a master plan, and then take a step-by-step approach. But the steps need to be taken more rapidly than at present, and they need to be taken with much more determination and purpose.

The first step will have to be admitting that we do not know how to build the future — then we need to start building it!

Made in the USA
Coppell, TX
27 February 2025

46477611R00105